BEAUTIFUL REBELLION

JOINING THE MOVEMENT TO CHANGE THE WORLD

BY BROCK MORGAN

DEDICATION

If you are not easily satisfied and you're longing for more,
then this book is for you.
It's for all of those dreamers looking for a better dream.
It's for the tender-hearted skeptics and doubters who haven't
lost their hope and are looking for more than the world is offering.
It's for the wide-eyed, faith-filled people who are looking for more
than what they are seeing in the church.
This book is for the storytellers in need of a better story.
It's for all of us who are desperate for the dawn to break.

THE SOUNDTRACK

I want to thank a few bands that have inspired me along the way as I've written. I love listening to music while I write. I find my mind and my typing work best when there's a beat.

So thank you to:

The Band CAMINO
Broods - *Don't Feed the Pop Monster*
Weezer - *Teal Album*
Alessia Cara - *The Pains of Growing*
Switchfoot - *Native Tongue*
Bob Marley and the Wailers - *Legend*
For King & Country - *Burn the Ships*
George Harrison - *All Things Must Pass*
Lauren Daigle - *Look Up Child*
Pearl Jam
Martin Smith – *Iron Lung*
Drew Holcomb and the Neighbors
Hawk House
Kendrick Lamar

CONTENTS

Every great dream begins with a dreamer.
Always remember, you have within you the
strength, the patience, and the passion to
reach for the stars to change the world.

-Harriet Tubman

1 | GENERATION Z READY

I walked out onto the arena's darkened stage as the video played. I set up behind the music stand and gathered my thoughts, preparing to speak to the crowd of thousands of teenagers. Suddenly, at the foot of the stage I noticed three teen girls. I leaned over to see what was happening. "Hey, what's up?" I asked. When I looked closer, I realized that all three were weeping. Without warning the stage lights came on, but there there girls stood, undeterred. I pushed my mic to the side, ignoring the crowd, and quietly asked again, "What's going on?" The middle girl got her composure. "We're desperate to know Jesus like you've been talking about all weekend," she said. I pointed to the corner of the stage. "I'll meet you over there as soon as I finish speaking tonight," I told them.

I've noticed something in teenagers today. They are dying for a life worth living. Like these three girls, they are longing for more. They want to be a part of something larger than themselves.

You wouldn't hear this from most adults who look at your generation from a distance. They call you Generation Z. Generation Z refers to people born from the late 1990s through the mid-2000s. A flurry of other potential labels have appeared, including Gen-Tech, post-Millennials, iGeneration, and Gen Wi-Fi. Adults look at your generation, see you on your phones, and think, "Is there really anything going on inside of them?!" And as with most things in life, these adults are judging you from afar. It's really easy to judge from the outside, isn't it? But if they just took some time to really see and really listen, they'd see and hear a very different story. A story of teenagers ready and waiting, 24/7. Longing for a movement.

Recently a teenager asked me to meet him for coffee. He comes every week to our youth group and we've been talking about being beautifully angry. To be beautifully angry is look out at the world and see what's wrong in it. There are certain things that make most of us pretty upset. We see the injustices, we see the broken and disregarded, and we think, "How in the world are we allowing this to happen?!" Living a life with beautiful anger means you're actually angry enough to want to do something about it. You are tired of sitting passively and you have to engage. I told this young man that I wanted to be beautifully angry for the rest of my life, crushing what is wrong in the world one issue at a time. I asked him to join me.

Now to be honest, I didn't really know him very well. He comes to youth group every week but he's quiet, or at least he's kind of quiet and withdrawn at our gatherings. But at this coffee shop, he couldn't stop talking.

"Brock, I've been plagued by what you were talking about, and I know what I want to give my life to. I go to a school where it seems like everyone is miserable. Everyone is stressed out, full of anxiety. No one feels safe to be themselves. It's like everyone is hiding, pretending, and they're consumed with getting out of here. They dream constantly of college, but they're unable to find joy right now."

I listened, encouraging him to continue. "Dude, I love what I'm hearing. This is beautiful!"

He went on. "Here's the thing. I feel powerless to change *anything*. I don't know what to do. Can you help me, because I can't sit back and just go with the flow of this whole thing. I've got to do something!"

I was stunned, excited, and well…overwhelmed. I wasn't sure I knew how to respond. We sat there in the silence for probably, um, way too long. I mean, heck, I'm a youth pastor. He was saying to me exactly what I've been praying to hear from a teenager for years. And still, I wasn't sure what to say. But then it came to me. "What if you and I start meeting every week?" I asked. "We could pray and dream and then start to invite your friends from school to join us in dreaming and praying and scheming? What if we started with just you? Every movement starts with the one. You could be the one."

I saw him come alive right in front of my eyes. "Yes. You bet. I'm in!"

I think this is actually the "I'm in" generation. When those in your generation see something worthy of giving your lives to, you're all in. You're ready, waiting, 24/7. But until then, well, it might seem like not much is happening.

For a number of years now I have had the privilege of traveling around the country speaking to teenagers at schools, camps, retreats, and conferences. It's one of my favorite things I get to do, besides being a youth pastor. At these events I get to talk about how Jesus has become a very real person in my life and how he has called me to give my life to this generation. Something interesting has happened, though, over the past five years. When I speak, I see a longing on teenagers' faces. I'm sensing something new and profound in them. It's like those three girls who said to me at the front of the stage, "Brock, we want to know Jesus like you've been talking about."

Now, you need to know something. I honestly believe that you are not reading this book by mistake. God has placed a dream within you. You are reading right now because there is a call on your life. God is waking you up to an incredible dream. He wants you to live with beautiful anger, for the rest of your life. Making a difference everywhere you go. The world is broken. It is lost. You know this. You know things are not working. The world is in need. Your friends are in need.

(And all together we yell a resounding "No duh!")

There's this great passage of Scripture in Romans that talks about how there is suffering in the world. It says that the whole of creation is basically trapped and waiting to get unstuck. What unsticks it? Well, this passage says that when the people of God rise up and take their place, a massive movement will happen. That there will be a generation who will get it, and when they are revealed, God himself will usher in something wonderful. Something we're all longing for. But until then, the plague will continue.

Here's the passage:

> I consider that our present sufferings are not worth comparing with the glory that will be revealed in us. For the creation waits in eager expectation for the children of God to be revealed.
>
> Romans 8:18-19

Years ago, a teenage guy named Ben Shive began to have a dream. He knew he was made for something bigger than the life he was living, and he knew God had gifted him in music. But how could he use his art to call a generation up and out and into something bigger than themselves?

One day he got together with his friend Andrew Peterson and they wrote a song called "Is He Worthy?" The song speaks about how this generation and all of creation are longing for something more, waiting for God to break through—and how God is actually going to do just that. Together they wrote this incredible song that Chris Tomlin ended up recording. Amazing!

I believe God is ready to break through, in and through us. Are you ready? I sure am. And I know those three girls from the foot of the stage are ready. I know that guy in my youth group is. I know all of his friends are. We are ready. Let's do this.

You could come with us, you know.
We need warriors and leaders like you.

-Enfys Nest, *Solo: A Star Wars Story*

2 | WELCOME TO THE REVOLUTION

I love rebellion movies!

The kind of movies where the world is broken, people are in bad shape, and those in power are evil and corrupt. But then a few rise up to fight against this backward, upside down, broken system to bring change, to right wrongs, and to usher in something fresh—renewal.

Movies like:
The Hunger Games
Solo
The Matrix
Ready Player One
Robin Hood

Robin Hood is kind of the classic example. I like the old cartoon Disney version a lot, but my favorite Robin Hood movie is the Kevin Costner and Morgan Freeman one from the 1990s.

In this telling of the story, the people of England are being exploited by the evil Sheriff of Nottingham when a young man's (Robin's) family is killed. Robin, like many of us would, gets angry. Angry enough to actually do something. He's not just angry at what has happened to his own family. He looks at his country, at the vulnerable poor. He sees the desperation in the people, and he's compelled to do something. Now, the "something" he lands on might be debatable to some, but I kind of like it.

Robin comes up with a plan to take money from the corrupt wealthy and give it to those who are starving and in need. Soon after he puts his plan into action, there is liberation for the people who were suffering.[1]

Or take *The Hunger Games*. In this story, as punishment for a past rebellion, the twelve districts of the nation of Panem are forced by the Capitol to select two tributes, one boy and one girl between twelve and eighteen years of age, to fight to the death in the annual Hunger Games. The Games end only when there is a single survivor.

Notice who is sacrificed every year: young people.

But in District 12, after her younger sister Primrose is chosen as tribute, Katniss Everdeen volunteers to take Primrose's place. What Katniss doesn't know is that the people are ripe for a new rebellion and her sacrifice is what will fuel it. Katniss becomes the very person to instigate a movement that liberates the entire nation.[2]

In the storyline of *The Matrix*, computer programmer Thomas Anderson is living a double life as a hacker named Neo. He feels like something is wrong with the world and is puzzled by repeated online encounters with cryptic mentions of "The Matrix." A woman named Trinity contacts him, saying that a man named Morpheus can explain its meaning. So Neo meets Morpheus, who offers him a choice between a red pill that will show him the truth and a blue pill that will return him to his delusional former life.

After swallowing the red pill, his reality disintegrates and Neo awakens in a liquid-filled pod, among countless others who are connected by cables to an elaborate electrical system where human beings act as batteries for the Matrix. He is rescued and brought aboard Morpheus's hovercraft, the *Nebuchadnezzar*.

The Matrix is a shared simulation of the world, in which the minds of all humans are trapped but also pacified. Morpheus and his crew are rebels who hack into the Matrix to "unplug" enslaved humans and call them into an awakened existence.[3]

It's quite an incredible idea that kind of rings true, huh?

I also love the movie *Ready Player One*. We own it and I watch it probably too much, but for some reason it just doesn't get old. It's about an orphaned teenager, Wade Watts. (Who, by the way, is born in 2027. That number is something you'll be seeing in this book quite a bit.) The story takes place in 2045, when much of humanity uses the virtual reality software OASIS to escape the desolation of the real world. Wade discovers clues to a hidden game within the program. Whoever wins this hidden game is promised full ownership of the OASIS. He joins several allies to try to complete the game before a large company can do so. I won't tell you the ending, but it's awesome![4]

The last one I want to mention is one of my all-time favorite movies: *Solo: A Star Wars Story*. The character of Han Solo is the classic example of someone who is made for a rebellion but doesn't know it. He's caught up in a system that he knows is wrong, but all he can think about is himself and what he wants. This is what the world he's living in is all about: selfish, self-centered power.

When Han Solo is awakened to a better story many years later, he joins the rebellion. Even though he seems like the person most likely *not* to join, he ends up being one of its main contributors.[5]

Many of us, like Han Solo, are living a status quo existence, but down deep we know something isn't right.

We are longing for a better story.

A bigger story.
An important story to be a part of.

But it seems like the Matrix is keeping us locked up, pacified and small.

The reason Hollywood tells these stories over and over again is because we are all hardwired to fight broken systems.

The crazy thing is that the ideas behind these movies are not far-fetched. It's not only in movies that you'll find teenagers rising up.

If you look, you'll find passionate young people in every era of history, who act as catalysts for change in the world.

In the real world, young people have always risen up and revolted. There have always been teenagers who have said, "Enough!" There have always been important moments when young people have been awakened to join a better story than what is being offered to them.

March for Our Lives
Students from Parkland, Florida, who faced a tragic shooting at their high school in February of 2018, organized March for Our Lives, a student-led demonstration to demand reasonable gun control legislation, which they hoped would end school shootings. It honestly doesn't matter if you agree or disagree with their thinking. Seeing teenagers rising up in an organized effort to bring change is inspiring.

These young people from Parkland aren't anomalies. They aren't even the newest link in a long chain of youth activists at the forefront of social change across the globe.

Right now, for instance, a movement among teenage girls is underway in China.

#MeToo
In China, the communist government is extremely controlling. China has its own Internet separate from the world's, with its own form of

Facebook and other social media, and the government controls all of it. No one can go on Twitter and like even a semi-negative statement about the government. People there live with a type of fear that has been normalized and accepted. On top of that, women in China have been abused and treated like second-class citizens. For decades, the Chinese government mandated what was known as a "one-child policy," restricting most urban families to one child. Because sons were valued more than daughters, female babies were often aborted. Can you imagine?

This kind of culture is crippling, especially for girls. A couple of years ago in the U.S. the #MeToo movement started. Somehow, a miracle happen and the movement reached China. Girls everywhere, even throughout China, were sharing their stories of horrific abuse. But the government was not happy, and China put a stop to all #MeToo posts on social media.

Then, a few teenage girls got an idea—a beautiful and rebellious idea. In Chinese the words *rice bunny* (pronounced "mi tu") sound like the English words *me too*. Out of this the Rice Bunny movement was birthed. Girls all over China, in mass rebellion, have continued confronting the abuse of girls (and more recently boys) with the #RiceBunny movement.

You can go back through the years and see movement after movement led by teenagers: The World War II Jitterbug movement (which was a teenage rebellion against Germany's policies that made black and Jewish music illegal, as well as other horrible atrocities), the civil rights movement of the 1960s, the anti-war movement of that same era, and many others.

Young people have always made inroads into culture. Again and again young people have seen the older generations getting it wrong, and so they've responded, making a massive cultural difference.

You can look at the Bible and see this played out over and over again. For example, there is this kid in the Bible named Isaiah. The world he lived in was in horrific shape. In his story, we not only discover what

Isaiah's heart is like, but we also see what God's heart is, not only for Isaiah, but for the world.

In Isaiah's time, the world is heading into a kind of living death that God wants humanity rescued from. The people of Israel have turned their backs on God. The rich are getting richer. The poor are not only getting poorer but are being taxed so that Israel can increase in power and secure its borders. On top of all of that, the Israelites have begun to worship a fertility goddess, whom they call The Queen of the Heavens. Her name is Ashtoreth.

Literally, the Israelites reject the God who rescued them from slavery. At one time, they were overwhelmed by his peace and blessings but even after all that God has done, they leave him and begin worshipping the goddess Ashtoreth, an Assyrian deity.

Now, let me tell you something cool about Assyria. Well, maybe not cool, but super interesting. At this time, Assyria is the most powerful and most influential nation in this area of the world. Powerful at this time can also be understood as warlike—they were brutal. The Assyrians conquered those they fought, and Assyrian culture became the dominant culture for all the surrounding people. You may have heard of their capital city, Nineveh.

Nineveh is the city from the Bible story known as Jonah and the Whale (a.k.a., really big fish). Jonah was sent to Nineveh to call the people there to repentance, but Jonah hated the Assyrians who lived in Nineveh. He hated them so much that he would rather die than go to them, which he tried to do several times, rather unsuccessfully. So this goddess, Ashtoreth, was straight out of the dominant culture of the time.

Now, the Assyrian culture was violent and oppressive. Ashtoreth demanded a terrible price for fertility. In order to appease her, children were given as temple prostitutes and many were ritually sacrificed. By sacrificing their young, the Israelites believed that Ashtoreth would bless them and protect them, giving them security, more children to care for them, and, of course, wealth.

The result was massive sexual brokenness, child abandonment, abuse, and rampant confusion with perversion ensuing.
The reality is that the people were afraid and miserable.

This was a very dark world, and God wanted to liberate all of them.

So God asks, "Who can I send?" This is where we get back to Isaiah. Let's take a look at the passage.

> In the year that King Uzziah died, I saw the Lord, high and exalted, seated on a throne; and the train of his robe filled the temple. Above him were seraphim, each with six wings: With two wings they covered their faces, with two they covered their feet, and with two they were flying. And they were calling to one another: "Holy, holy, holy is the Lord Almighty; the whole earth is full of his glory."
> At the sound of their voices the doorposts and thresholds shook and the temple was filled with smoke.
> "Woe to me!" I cried. "I am ruined! For I am a man of unclean lips, and I live among a people of unclean lips, and my eyes have seen the King, the Lord Almighty."
> Then one of the seraphim flew to me with a live coal in his hand, which he had taken with tongs from the altar. With it he touched my mouth and said, "See, this has touched your lips; your guilt is taken away and your sin atoned for."
> Then I heard the voice of the Lord saying, "Whom shall I send? And who will go for us?"
> And I said, "Here am I. Send me!"
>
> Isaiah 6:1-8

What we may not realize about this passage right away is that in it, God is calling Isaiah into a revolution, a rebellion. What a heavy call God is placing on young Isaiah. This is flat-out overwhelming. Because this story is not just about believing in God, but actually following God into the darkest of places to rescue people and change a system. This is beyond heavy.

God asks, "Who will actually go for me and rescue humanity?"

Who will restore dignity to women and children?

Who will care for the poor?
Who will stand up for the hurting and the powerless?
Who will invite people back into relationship with me?

This is the heart of God.

"Who will I send?"

And we see that Isaiah, without hesitation, says, "Send me." This
might be the most shocking part of the story. But it's the only way the
movement God wants to bring about can actually happen.

When faith in God is finally lived out, it requires boots. It requires
action.
It actually brings justice.
It rights wrongs.
It banishes evil.
It stands for beauty and calls out the best in people.
It is deeply in tune with God's Spirit.
It's wholistic. It cares for the whole: mind, spirit, body.
Isaiah recognizes this enough to say to God, "Send me."

In this book I'm asking you to really consider what opening your life
to Jesus might look like.

But you need to know that this is a really BIG ask. Our world is
broken and this rebellion needs warriors and leaders like you.
I honestly believe that if you open yourself to him in a deeper way,
you'll actually hear God calling you into a new rebellion, just like
Isaiah did.
A whole new way of thinking and living.

Because faith is a movement.

*A coward is incapable of exhibiting love;
it is the prerogative of the brave.*

-Mahatma Gandhi

3 | THERE IS A CRISIS

I was looking through some of the best professional photos taken so far this year. They are stunning, taken by world-renowned photographers who happened to be in the right place at the right time. Some of these pictures are beautiful and inspiring.
But most are tragic.
Violent.
Difficult.
Scary.
Depressing.

Recently, an awesome teenage girl asked to meet with me after one of my talks at youth group. She was smiling and happy and so I thought the conversation would be, well, a smiley, happy one. But when she started to tell me what she was going through, it was anything but. As soon as she started to share, her facial expression changed and tears welled up in her eyes. It was like she finally felt free to stop pretending.

She said, "Brock, I've been having massive anxiety problems lately. It's killing me and I'm not sure I can go on. I know I can't go on. If something doesn't change, I won't go on."

She said something I think a lot of us can relate to. We know the world is broken. You can turn the news on for one minute, or better yet, walk the hallways of a local school, or listen to a teenager after youth group, and you'll know things aren't right.

Right now, we are all more aware of the brokenness in the world than generations before us have been. We see the direction we are going. But many of us don't know what to do about it. We think, "It just is this way, I guess."

But all of this is connected to Jesus's words when he said that there are two ways. Look at this passage with me for a moment:

> Enter through the narrow gate. For wide is the gate and broad is the road that leads to destruction, and many enter through it. But small is the gate and narrow the road that leads to life, and only a few find it.
> Matthew 7:13-14

So what Jesus is really saying is there are only two ways to live, or two roads to live on.
The wide road and the narrow road. Just two. That's it.

Now, surprisingly, Jesus says the wide road is the road the leads to destruction.

Let me tell you what destruction looks like in our culture:
It's anxiety.
It's addiction.
It's the kind of fear that grips you and won't let go.
It's in schools when bullying happens, when exclusion occurs.

That's what Jesus is talking about when he talks about destruction. It means having a miserable existence. That's the wide road most of us are on.

Did you know that your generation, Generation Z, is the most medicated, anxiety-ridden, and addicted generation in history?[6-9]

This is incredibly alarming.

Why your generation?
Why would there be such brokenness, hurt, confusion, and addiction?
And why does it all feel so normal?

Did you know that since 2011, suicide attempts among teenage boys have gone up 25%?
Did you know that since 2011, suicide attempts among teenage girls have gone up 70%?[10, 11]

Wide is the way that leads to destruction.
Destruction is the opposite of wholeness.

Many of us view God as some kind of killjoy. He is all about rules that cramp our style and steal our fun. But the reality is, he really wants you to thrive.
He doesn't want you riddled by anxiety.
He wants you to be passionate, not haunted by apathy.
He wants you healthy in mind and body.
He doesn't want you to fall into any form of addiction or brokenness.

He wants you to thrive!

This makes me think of my friend Karen. Karen is awesome for so many reasons. She is a world record holder in triathlons, plus she is just an amazing person. She outruns, out-swims, and out-bikes people from all over the world, and she's done all of this while battling cancer. Remarkable! But she is also deathly afraid of the ocean. She won't get in—like, at all.

One day she stopped me in the lobby of our church. "Brock, have I got a story for you!" she said. I love a good story and I love Karen, so I was all in.

"We just got back from vacation in Hawaii and I was afraid to get in the ocean pretty much the whole time. We were there for ten days and the first nine days I just sat on the beach dying to get in. But I was just way too scared to do it," she said. "I'd watch my husband and my kids out there playing and body surfing and snorkeling, but I just couldn't get past my ankles in the water. Brock, honestly, I was miserable. I was completely gripped by fear."

"On the last full day that we were there, I was standing at the edge of the water praying that God would give me the courage to finally get in. I prayed that he would take this overwhelming fear away from me. I kid you not, I sensed God speak to me in a very clear way. He said, 'Karen, just get in and I'll swim with you.' All of a sudden something rammed my foot in the water." She grinned. "Well, I started jumping and screaming and immediately ran out of the water. But then I thought, no, let me just put my feet in again."

She looked at me. "In that moment I heard God say again, 'Get in, I'll swim with you.' So I put my feet in and I looked down and there was this little six-inch blue fish right at my feet. And it swam into my ankle again."

"Oh my gosh Karen, what did you do? Run out again?" I asked, smiling.

"Yep," she said. "But it made me super curious. So I ran into the house we were staying at and grabbed my snorkel gear. You know, the snorkel gear that I hadn't used the entire time we were there."

"I stood there at the water's edge again, this time with my feet not in the water, and I sensed God again say, 'Get in, I'll swim with you.' So I started to walk out into the deeper water and all of a sudden something softly bumped me in the chest. And instead of feeling overwhelmed with fear, I sensed the presence of God. Brock, I felt nothing but courage and a strange calm came over me. I felt peace." I was amazed. "Karen," I said, "this is amazing!"

"Oh, you haven't heard anything yet," she said. "I put my snorkel mask on and put my face under the water and there it was, the cutest blue fish that you have ever seen!"

"It sounds like Dory, from *Finding Nemo*."

"Yep, exactly. I was swimming with Dory," she said with a smile. "But it wasn't Dory. In that moment I again sensed God say, 'Karen, come on, let's swim together.' This little fish and I began swimming together, exploring the beautiful coral reef and we watched other fish swimming by." I shook my head in amazement. "This little fish would come and kiss me on my face from time to time. He would kiss me on my cheek and then the other cheek and then my forehead and then we'd swim a bit and he'd come back and kiss me again and again. We swam together for hours. I didn't want to get out. We swam together and I was smiling and crying, and laughing all at the same time. Brock, God swam with me!"

I was blown away. Karen is not the kind of person to make something like this up. Her story is remarkable. And it sounds so much like Jesus to me. It shows so much about who he is and what he wants for us.

God's heart is for you to know who you really are—
that you are
loved.
adored.
That you have a purpose.
That you're made to be in relationship with deep-spirited friends.
You're made to be in close relationship with him.
He wants you to be whole.
He is with you.
He wants to free you from fear.
Fear of the water.
Fear of the future.
Fear of being yourself.
Fear of not fitting in.
Fear of never finding what you are meant for.
He is with you.
All of the brokenness in the world is the result of a culture heading in

the wrong direction. Living on the wrong road. It's obvious that the way we are living and the direction we are going aren't working. They just aren't. They aren't working!

We have student leadership at my church youth group. It's full of the most passionate people you've ever met. They have been captured by this passage of Scripture in Romans. Check it out:

> So here's what I want you to do, God helping you: Take your everyday, ordinary life—your sleeping, eating, going-to-work, and walking-around life—and place it before God as an offering. Embracing what God does for you is the best thing you can do for him. Don't become so well-adjusted to your culture that you fit into it without even thinking. Instead, fix your attention on God. You'll be changed from the inside out. Readily recognize what he wants from you, and quickly respond to it. Unlike the culture around you, always dragging you down to its level of immaturity, God brings the best out of you, develops well-formed maturity in you.
>
> Romans 12:1-2 (MSG)

One day our student leadership team was reading this passage together. I went to the white board and asked, "What does this mean for us?" We started brainstorming. Here's what we came up with:

- We live life together in community—which means on-purpose, everyday encouragement and loving accountability.
- We never struggle alone! If we do, we have failed.
- The world is going one way and that way ain't working!
- We can redefine play and fun for teens today. We don't need drugs and the party scene to have a great time. Let's redefine fun for our generation.
- God will help us creatively live remarkable lives in our schools.
- He is so with us!
- God wants us to grow. All we have to do is say yes to him and to each other.

I was so proud that they were actually getting it!

What they were describing represents a true uprising. A rebellion against the way things are. A movement to a new way.

A bunch of young people getting out of the current everyone else is riding. Realizing that we need a different way. That the way things are isn't working. In fact, the way things are is killing us.

These young people are ready, and I have a feeling they aren't the only ones. I have a feeling that a movement, a beautiful rebellion, might be coming.

The greatest crimes in the world are not committed by people breaking the rules but by people following the rules.
It's people who follow orders that drop bombs and massacre villages.

–Banksy, *Wall and Piece*

4 | BEAUTIFUL REBELLION

I have the privilege of speaking to middle school, high school, and college students from every corner of this country. It's a huge honor, honestly. And I love it! I think I feel this way because I believe a big part of my calling is to wake this generation up. So many people today seem to be heroes without a mission. Think about that: a superhero who knows she has power but doesn't see a role for herself in a world like the one we live in.

Over the past ten years, one my favorite Bible passages has become Ephesians 5. Look at these verses with me. Maybe circle some words or phrases that jump out at you:

> For you were once darkness, but now you are light in the Lord. Live as children of light (for the fruit of the light consists in all goodness, righteousness and truth) and find out what pleases the Lord. Have nothing to do with the fruitless deeds of darkness, but rather expose them. It is shameful even to mention what the disobedient do in secret. But everything exposed by the light becomes

visible—and everything that is illuminated becomes a light.
This is why it is said:
"Wake up, oh sleeper,
rise from the dead,
and Christ will shine on you."

Ephesians 5:8-14

I think it's really interesting that these verses call us "darkness." They don't say that we were *in* darkness, but that we *were* darkness. Think about that. You and I *were* darkness.

But then it says, "Now, you *are* light." This is a completely new identity. Something has shifted. You are light. This is who you are. Your very presence lights up dark places.
You.
The one who struggles.
The one who feels lost at times.
The one who's afraid.
The one who keeps messing up.
You.
You are light.

This is a radical redefinition of who you are, and it flies in the face of what you've been told. When we define ourselves by our mistakes or even our temporary successes, we're believing in a false self. It's darkness. It's not true. It isn't who you are. Your good or bad grades don't make or break you.
You are light. That's it.
And because of that, you have a vital role to play.
You get to light up dark places.

Then the passage says that in order to light things up, you must wake up. You've got to be awake in order to do what you were created for. And when you wake up, Jesus will shine on you. That's crazy! This is LIGHT shining on light. Jesus the Light shines on us who are light. Insane!

But the thing is, in the passage it basically says that the light is asleep.

We, who are light, are sleeping. We are allowing the darkness to reign. We're like those superheroes who don't know their purpose. Something has to change. There's got to be a massive wake-up. There must be a great awakening! And in order for that to actually happen, a rebellion must take place.

In every rebellion, there are stages or steps. I'm not talking about rebelling against your mom when she asks you to put your phone away. You feel that anger inside bubble up and your temperature rising. You yell, "You put yours away first!"

No, I'm talking about a beautiful rebellion. I'm talking about an organized rebellion, a movement that challenges the systems that are not for the common good. The kind of rebellion I'm talking about is a liberation. Liberation can *only* come out of rebellion. Pushing back against the way things are in order to establish a better way.

Stages of a Rebellion
1. Rejecting identity, circumstances, situations, or cultural norms
2. Defining a new and desired identity and set of circumstances/norms
3. Taking a stand and seeking liberation
4. Ongoing resistance
5. Establishing a new way[12]

Reading this list gets me excited because I'm ready for mass change. We really need it! But how do we make good change happen on a big scale and in a way that lasts? Understanding the stages of a rebellion can help. Let's dive a little deeper into what they look like.

1. Rejecting Identity, Circumstances, Situations, or Cultural Norms
What identity has culture given your generation? How have you been labeled and boxed in? What do "they" say you are?

Lazy? Entitled? Anxiety-ridden? Selfish? Fearful? Too sensitive? Addicted? Can't live without your cell phones?

I say no! That's not who you really are. That's not what God sees!

We need an organized and determined rejection of these lies: "This is not who we are! We are more than our habits, our problems, our struggles, our sexuality, and our fears!"

Now to be fair, there can be, and often is, truth behind any label. When I was in tenth grade, for example, I walked into a conversation between some students in the hallway of my school. They were talking about who at school was a virgin. It was a strange conversation to walk into; it's not every day you approach people and hear them say, "Jonny is a virgin and so is Sally." The students talking were pretty religious and active in their youth group. So naturally I walked up and blurted out, "Hey, I'm a virgin too."

They looked at me with the most judgmental eyes. It was actually a bit jarring! They said, "Yeah, maybe technically you are, but we've heard what you've been into lately, dude, and you're kind of a hypocrite."

I was stunned. Frozen where I stood. I made some excuse and headed out with my head down. I exited the hallway feeling embarrassed, belittled, misunderstood, and humiliated. But I also knew there was some truth to what they were saying. This moment was kind of a game changer for me. I realized I hadn't been thoughtful with my choices. I was hanging out with a group of people who were going down a very different path than I really wanted to go down. Deep inside, I knew the students talking in the hallway were right about me. I was a hypocrite. And I needed to make serious changes in my life. I needed to decide who I really was and how I wanted to treat girls.

In the Scriptures, God tells us over and over again who we really are. Even in the midst of our sin, our rebellion against God, and our apathy, he's like, "No, that's not who you really are. You are holy. You're beautiful and you've been set apart for an incredible life." I love what it says in 1 Peter 2:

> But you are a chosen people, a royal priesthood,
> a holy nation, God's special possession, that you
> may declare the praises of him who called you out of

darkness into his wonderful light.

1 Peter 2:9

That "But" is huge. Ha! Seriously though, we need to pay attention to it. The first word in that verse is super important because we tend to come to God with every excuse in the book. And he simply says, "Yeah, I know that, BUT this is who I say you are."

We say, "I've made really bad choices."
God says, "But you are chosen. But I've picked you."

We say, "I'm a mess."
God says, "But actually, you are royal because you're my child."

We say, "I belong to a broken family, and all of my friends are going in a totally different direction than I want to."
God says, "But see, you belong to me. You are meant for freedom. You are my kid and with that comes an incredible life."

God always answers our excuses with a big "but." The question is this:

Will we reject the circumstances and situations and identities that are shaping us in a way that's opposite from what God's vision is for us? Once we realize that these other identities and habits and ways of thinking and seeing are actually robbing from us, it becomes a no brainer to embrace and join this much-needed rebellion. As God's children, we then become his rebel leaders.

2. Defining a New and Desired Identity and Set of Circumstances
A movement—a rebellion—begins with rejecting that old stuff that isn't part of what God wants for us and then, secondly, holding fast to this new dream of God's, this new desired outcome. A movement pushes us into a completely different kind of future.
Because you are the selfless generation.
You are the compassionate ones.
You are hungry for freedom for yourself and for others.
You are creative.
You are the ones who are dying for a life worth living! This is the new you.

3. Taking a Stand and Seeking Liberation

I recently heard from a friend that San Francisco Bay-area teenagers are moving away from smartphones *en masse*. They don't want them. The cool thing, for thousands of these California kids, is a flip phone. I have to admit, I loved my old flip phone. These Bay Area teens have read research on how addictive smartphones are and they see their parents constantly on their phones. And so in rebellion, they are rejecting iPhones and Androids. I find it a cool movement toward liberation.

Taking a stand for real change just might require something of us. We want to be liberated, but many of us like the cages we have built around ourselves. Maybe we like our smartphones. But a movement can't happen until we leave these cages, moving toward whatever it is that will liberate us.

What might a movement look like for you, for us? I can picture teenagers all over the world starting campaigns to change the school systems that do little more than create cultures of anxiety, pushing back against the destructive forces that corrupt love and numb our minds. I can see teenagers everywhere calling their friends into the best and most freeing lives possible, lives that crave the closeness of Jesus. Lives that embrace spirituality and that reject old and stale religion. This sounds like a beautiful rebellion to me.

This generation could actually do something!

4. Ongoing Resistance

For a movement to be sustainable, there has to be endurance. This is the hard work of leaning into change, not losing hope, and believing that the change we are struggling to bring about is imperative for the good of humanity. What would it mean to be organized and begin a movement that doesn't run out of steam, like so many of us do a week after camp or a mission trip? Dr. Martin Luther King, Jr., gave a speech titled "Remaining Awake Through a Great Revolution" to the graduating class of Oberlin College in 1965. In it, he conveys the thought that we can actually miss what we're meant to be a part of. We can fall asleep and never enter in to the great calling God has given us, the calling to bring hope and freedom to the marginalized. We have to be vigilant because of the roadblocks set before us. As Dr. King said in this speech, "With this faith we will be able to hew out of the mountain of despair, the stone of hope."[13] It's because of this hope that I picture teenagers changing the structures of their youth groups. I can see them telling their youth pastors, "We want to do the teaching, we want to lead, let us run with this thing. Let's have a night of worship and a day of service. Let's truly get to know our neighbors and bless them. Let's change all of the meaningless busyness and get serious about what it truly means to be salt and light in our communities."

5. Establishing a New Way

Movements that have true success create new norms, new patterns, and new ways of thinking. The Scriptures actually address this, recognizing that lip service is not enough. Really establishing a new way happens through transforming the mind and how we think, which leads us into action. Romans 12:2 (NET) says, "Do not be conformed to this present world, but be transformed by the renewing of your mind, so that you may test and approve what is the will of God—what is good and well-pleasing and perfect." This changes everything! Because if you know who you truly are, who God says you are, you will act out of that love and security.

When I was in third grade, my parents wanted me to become a runner. My mom, who is an over-the-top encourager, told me, "Brock, you are such a fast runner. I love to watch you run." At that age you believe what you are told, so I had no doubt that I was, indeed, a fantastic runner. I ran as fast as I could. Amazingly, I competed in the Junior Olympics a few years later. Here is the truth, though. I was not necessarily the fastest runner—but I believed I was. I had no reason to doubt my mom, who loved me and thought the very best of me. I was a runner. I was fast. Watching me run brought her joy. A new way had been established in my thinking, which translated to my actions.

We too are runners in a different kind of race. And we must fight for this new way and allow God to capture our minds. Let him whisper words of healing, truth, strength, freedom, and belonging into your ear, and let them transform your thinking. Let them translate into how you choose to live. Let the rebellion against those things that cause brokenness in yourself, in your friends, and in your family flourish as you set your eyes on him.

As You Reflect on All of This, Here Are Some Questions to Think Through
- What stands out to you about the stages of rebellion?
- How have you personally experienced the brokenness of the world?
- What do you think God's heart is for what hurts you and others?

All of this can sound kind of overwhelming, I know. But the reality is that God has a dream. A dream for a generation to rise up. For that generation to take its place, to lead us back to hope and life and peace and love.

We all see that our culture's direction isn't heading into life. But God is hoping to see a generation rise up and move against the flow.

I think you just might be part of the perfect generation for this, and for good reason.

Your generation is hard-wired for passion. Now, I realize you can look at some young people and have good reason to think that there's more passion in a fern than there is in them. But the reality is that just below the surface for most of us is a massive amount of emotion and feeling and desire.

Second, **you are less fearful than older generations who are stuck.** The early church was led by young people—*almost exclusively!* Why? Because they weren't stuck like the older adults: stuck in their religions and the systems they had grown comfortable with. You are made to be a difference-maker! Young people haven't lost the ability to see that and act on it.

Third, **you don't have as strong a sense of consequence.** Now, this is at times can be a really bad thing. Like that time my friend, when we were sixteen years old, jumped out of a moving bus, only to SPLAT on the ground. (He was fine, by the way.) What was he thinking? Well, he wasn't!

But here's the truth. So many young people don't know the outcome of, or spend a lot of time worrying about, the impact of certain decisions. This leads to really bad outcomes sometimes, but it also opens them up to live BIG lives, making massive impact.

Fourth, **you have a capacity to dream big dreams.** You have not been so damaged that you've stopped dreaming. The dreams you have for your life and for the world are God-sized dreams. You might not know exactly what your life will look like, BUT down deep you have a longing to do something meaningful, something significant. This longing has been gifted and placed inside of you by God himself!

Fifth, **God placed rebellion in you as a gift to help redeem the world.** Rebellion has typically been looked upon as bad. But I have to tell you, the desire for it has been given to you by God. The current of the culture is pulling everyone toward a small existence, and that's not what God wants for us. You were made for a beautiful rebellion that will take you away from anything that is stealing life, purpose, and meaning!

I really believe that your generation will see the world's story changed. And I believe your generation is vital to making those changes happen.

So,
What is God calling you to do?
What battle should you be fighting?
What injustice should you be righting?
What evil should you be banishing?
What revolution should you be joining?
This calling has been planted in you by God himself.
But here's the thing.
Before we storm the castle, God has something he wants to do with you.

He wants to fill you with his Spirit.
He wants to heal your brokenness.
He wants to comfort you.
He wants to restore you.
He wants to fill you with hope!
He wants to have a voice in your life.
He wants to tell you who you really are.

Rebel children, I urge you, fight the turgid slick of conformity with which they seek to smother your glory.

–Russell Brand, *My Booky Wook*

5 | SURPRISED BY NUMBERS

We were sitting there a couple of years back, late one night in a London pub, when my friend looked at me. "Hey, Brock, no worries man, just ten more years!" he said.

"Ten more years until what?" I asked.

"Just ten more till a movement starts. A major shift is coming, man."

I've always been skeptical of statements like this, but this one really got my attention, in part because of who said it. The friend I was talking to really understood culture. So I asked him to tell me more. He said the States have always been about twenty years behind the U.K. because of its conservative roots and how young the country is. But with the dawn of the Internet age and social media, he sees us in the States as lagging behind them only about ten years. And that's a good thing, because a movement has been happening in post-Christian Europe for a few years now. Thousands and thousands of young people are coming to Jesus and bringing change everywhere they go. My friend believed that kind of change was bound to follow in the U.S. "Dude," he said, "it's just around the corner, hang in there."

When Mark Oestreicher, my publisher (I call him Marko), asked me to think about writing another book, I couldn't get this conversation with my U.K. buddy out of my mind. It has absolutely gripped me for the better part of two years. *"Just ten more years, man!"*

I've been praying for a movement for over twenty-eight years of youth ministry. And when I say a movement, I don't mean a great week at camp followed by a slow dwindling back into normalcy. What I'm thinking of is more like God doing such remarkable work in and through us that, when we come home from camp, our communities are literally never the same. Our schools and homes and, please God, our churches see mass transformation.

A few years back when I wrote the book *Youth Ministry in a Post-Christian World*, I explained that the U.S. is heading into a period where the primary voices and influences will no longer be Christian. I can confidently say that we are currently in the midst of this time. You know this as a young person. Having doubts about faith is the norm for your generation. Teenagers aren't buying the church's easy answers any longer, and they shouldn't. Have you seen this in yourself?

It's like this: You have serious questions and your natural inclination might be to just accept what the church has kind of spoon-fed you. But deeper down, you really want to know what's actually true. Your generation's doubt is not a digging-your-heels-in-the-ground, unmovable, already-determined kind of doubt. It makes me think of what I've seen in the Bible in the story of this awesome guy named Thomas. This generation's doubt is a Thomas kind of doubt. He was one of Jesus's disciples and something happened that caused him to have serious #fomo.

All of the other disciples saw Jesus raised from the dead. But Thomas wasn't there to see this for himself. After it happened, all of the other disciples were freaking out and celebrating. Thomas walks in and is flabbergasted by what they are saying. He just can't believe them. It sounds crazy! Jesus rose from the dead?!

Well, it *was* crazy. And the thing about Thomas is that he really loved Jesus and he wanted to believe, but first he needed to see and experience Jesus for himself. He wanted to know firsthand what his friends knew. He needed it to be personal for him as well.

Have you ever felt that way? Your friend has this remarkable experience with God, which is awesome, but you'd like to have something similar for yourself? This was Thomas. This is your generation. Quick to doubt but at the same time very willing and open to know truth for yourselves.

Which brings me back to my phone call with my publisher. When I got off the phone with Marko, I had the idea for writing a book about a movement. A movement that actually gets launched by this Thomas generation, soon, within ten years. And then, as I was thinking about the idea, something kind of cool happened. I'm not sure if it was luck, mere coincidence, or the very hand of God.

It was 2017 when we had this conversation. "Hmm," I thought. "In ten years it will be 2027. Huh. That kind of has a ring to it." Then I thought, "I wonder if the story of Thomas being moved from doubt to faith and then into a movement is in a gospel near chapter 20 verse 27. That would be beyond cool."

So I opened my Bible to John 20:27 and there it was:

> Then Jesus focused his attention on Thomas. "Take your finger and examine my hands. Take your hand and stick it in my side. Don't be unbelieving. Believe."
> John 20:27 (MSG)

What?! Now, I'm not a "signs" guy. Well, okay, yes, I kind of am. This one, though, really got my attention. It was like God was with me in my idea. *What if God really wants to see a movement happen?* I wondered. *What if this is his heart?* This idea has started me on a journey of writing and traveling the country, trying to instigate this very movement. What I've found is that Generation Z is wide open and ready for it.

My guess is that if you're reading this book, it means that you and I share the same heart. You would love for God to move you from doubt to faith and into a movement. Or maybe you have already been moved into belief, but you're waiting and praying for something more. That's exactly where I am.

You, like me, are longing for God to do a new thing. And after spending a couple of years of wrestling with this, I can tell you that I'm all in. My belief is that this new thing we're being called into is the very dream of God. He sees the cry of our hearts and he sees the brokenness of the world and how Generation Z is ripe for this beautiful rebellion.

Before I get carried away, I do want to say: As you've probably noticed by now, this isn't a weird end times book, a prophetic word book, or any other weird cult-like reading. I believe it's just a call back to what God is longing to do in and through us. It's a call to wake up to what God is already doing, and to simply join him. He has already shown himself in transformative ways to a few, as he did to those disciples in that small room. But the masses sit like Thomas, ready for a firsthand, Jesus-y kind of change.

God is on the move. Are you ready, like Thomas, to see for yourself? Are you ready for Jesus to lead you into the often uncomfortable yet thrilling reality of his presence and calling?

> Then Jesus focused his attention on Thomas. "Take your finger and examine my hands. Take your hand and stick it in my side. Don't be unbelieving. Believe."
>
> John 20:27 (MSG)

Everybody is a genius. But if you judge a fish by its ability to climb a tree, it will live its whole life believing that it is stupid.

–Albert Einstein

6 | BIG BRAINS

One night at youth group when I was in tenth grade, in the middle of the youth pastor's talk, my friend and I got the giggles. We started laughing and we just could not stop. We had no idea what we were even laughing at. I bit my tongue really hard trying to get myself to stop, or keep it at least kind of quiet, but to no avail. Eventually one of us burst out loud with an explosion of laughter. The whole room full of teenagers and leaders turned to look at us like we were absolute morons. Which we were—but it was so much fun, you know? I love those moments, and as an adult I still crack up from time to time in our church staff meetings.

Last night I was sitting behind a little boy in our church's Saturday evening service. He was going crazy, crawling around on the floor, wiggling the chairs around. All of the sudden the folding chair he was halfway sitting on folded up on him. It was absolutely incredible. Unfortunately this kid started screaming in terror. The adults around me were obviously upset at his parents for allowing him to be such a distraction, their faces all scrunched up in disapproving looks. But

I flat-out loved the moment of nonsense. And I loved him! That kid is me. I started laughing out loud and I couldn't stop. It was the best church service I've been to in a really long while, thanks to the kid who wasn't made to sit still.

I even kind of enjoy it when things like this happen at youth group. I've never seen a teen get folded up into a chair, but you know how it goes. When teenagers get the giggles in the middle of one of my talks, I want to be part of the fun. I want in on it!

Now back to my tenth grade laughing fit. My friend and I were doing our best to calm down, making sure we didn't make eye contact with each other for the rest of the talk for fear that the laughter would emerge all over again. But afterward our youth pastor asked to meet with both of us.

I remember this super clearly. We were standing in the church kitchen away from everyone as our youth pastor began to express his disappointment in our behavior. Out of nowhere, my friend interrupted. "Look man, I don't even believe this stuff and I probably won't even be coming back here anymore!"

I was shocked. First we were laughing hysterically, then we were being lectured, and now my friend was unexpectedly revealing something real: He was no longer a Christian. My youth pastor stood there, seemingly unfazed. I, on the other hand, was absolutely floored— floored at what my friend had said, and floored that our youth pastor didn't seem upset. *I* was upset.

I went home that night questioning what I really believed. I wondered if my friend was right, if all of this faith stuff was nonsense. His doubt is what made me confront my own doubt. It forced me to dig deep, to clear away everything I could in order to find out if there was something, anything, still there worth building my life on. It ended up being the breaking apart of the soil where later a foundation would be laid for the days and years to come.

When my friend said, in his own way, that he was no longer a

Christian, it sent me on a personal discovery of truth that has continued to this very day. I was initially upset by what he said. The questions I started asking myself as a result of what he shared felt like betrayals of my family and of my church, and I kept them secret for a few months. It just didn't feel safe to admit what I was wondering. It felt wrong to question. I struggled in isolation until I couldn't stand it any longer.

One evening, my father and I went for a long ride in the car. I finally blurted everything out, confessing all of my doubts and questions and disbelief. His response threw me, in an unexpected and beautiful way. "Oh good, Brock!" he exclaimed. "I've been waiting for you to begin the digging process. I was wondering when those awesome questions would bubble up to the surface." When he said those words, complete relief poured over me. It felt like the beginning of a long holiday, like the first day of summer vacation.

As a child I was a believer. I'd leave church having heard those great stories in the Scriptures, feeling so amazed by who Jesus was and what he did. I loved listening to the pastor tell stories of miracles, and I experienced God personally in profound ways, even as a little guy. But it was a naive faith, and now I was growing up and needed to move to a more thoughtful and sophisticated one, with nuance.

Our culture is complex, full of really smart people who have differing perspectives and worldviews. At that point in my life I needed a deeper understanding of these complexities and beautiful subtleties, and humility that would help me as I headed out into the grown-up world.

The truth is that the American church, for the most part, doesn't like questions, especially the loaded ones many teenagers are asking. Questions often make church people feel uncomfortable, uneasy, and afraid that they might lead themselves and others into doubt and, ultimately, a rejection of faith. But that's not what your questions actually do. The questions many people fear are the very things that can lead to a faith that's wholistic and profound. Now, I have seen doubt do the opposite when it is experienced in isolation, away from humble, patient, and experienced adults who are like tour guides, pointing out things that teenagers would have otherwise missed. But many teenagers don't feel safe to express these questions, so they hide them away. From the adult perspective, when teens finally get to a point where they can no longer keep these thoughts or doubts or their lost faith to themselves, it can seem that they are bursting forth all of the sudden and out of nowhere.

A couple of years ago one of our teens got a part-time job. He had gone to our summer camp in DC, where he had an encounter with the Lord. Soon after camp, though, this part-time job kept him from coming regularly to youth group. A couple of months of his inconsistent attendance had gone by when I set up a time to reconnect. Over coffee he told me that he was looking deeper into Buddhism and that the Christian faith just wasn't making sense to him anymore. I dug a little deeper and found out that the things he was troubled by when it came to Christianity also troubled me. You likely know what those things are: hypocrisy, judgmental attitudes, the way many churches treat gay people, how political the American church has become, how today's churches don't resemble the early church movement, and on and on.

He was shocked that I understood his concerns. "What was it about Christian faith that initially drew you in?" I asked. As he started to share, I saw him begin to remember what he'd once connected with. The more he shared, the more I saw him strengthened. By the end of the conversation he had decided to change his work schedule so that he wouldn't miss youth group as much.

His life didn't dramatically change overnight. It was a journey. He finished that year regularly coming to youth group, and he came on our camps and mission trip. He was fully engaged in the journey. Over that year he kept asking questions, beautiful questions. And these questions caused him to build a strong foundation for his faith. I have absolutely loved watching him go through this. Currently he's a college student, serving as a leader at youth group. It is super cool seeing him helping other people grow.

Doubt in isolation is never good, but doubt in community can lead to a deepening of faith. The questions you have, if handled well, might be the very things that bring you and others into faith that has surprising depth and breadth.

I was talking with a former youth group kid two days ago. She's incredibly smart, now a freshman at Duke. She's the kind of person who does math in her free time. Can you believe that?! Math for fun. But not only is she smart, she also has a wonderful heart. We talked about the doubt that she has been dealing with as a freshman at Duke and some of the big life questions. During our conversation I looked at her and said, "If you can hang in there, and keep wrestling with these difficult questions, you will become dangerous. If you allow your questions to take you into deeper thinking, and if you go through that in community, then you will be powerful in the lives of people who need intellectual understanding in order to believe the gospel of Jesus." She looked back at me. "Yes! That's what I need," she said. "I've always thought doubt was the enemy, but I just really want to know what's true. If Jesus is the way, I want to know why, and then I want to help people find the truth."

Yes! That's it!

For a movement to have a lasting impact, it not only needs heart and passion and experiences with God's Spirit, but it also needs really big brains, like hers.

Start by doing what's necessary; then do what's possible; and suddenly you are doing the impossible.

–St. Francis of Assisi

7 | A GUY NAMED THOMAS
The beautiful journey from doubt to belief to a movement

As I wrote earlier, Thomas is one of my favorite characters in the Bible. His questions and his doubts were not rebuffed by Jesus. Instead, they set him up to further his journey into radical faith.

My wife, Kelsey, has a seminary professor from India. He was born and raised in a region called Kerala. Kerala is one of the only regions in India that has a long history of Christianity. In fact, that history in Kerala goes back a couple thousand years—and that's because of my favorite doubter-turned-missionary, Thomas. Thomas hit the road and began telling everyone about his risen friend Jesus, because of a turning point that moved him from skepticism to being willing to die for the faith.

Let's quickly look together at this story about Thomas:

> Now Thomas (also known as Didymus), one of the Twelve, was not with the disciples when Jesus came. So the other

disciples told him, "We have seen the Lord!"
But he said to them, "Unless I see the nail marks in his
hands and put my finger where the nails were, and put my
hand into his side, I will not believe."
A week later his disciples were in the house again, and
Thomas was with them. Though the doors were locked,
Jesus came and stood among them and said, "Peace be
with you!" Then he said to Thomas, "Put your finger here;
see my hands. Reach out your hand and put it into my side.
Stop doubting and believe."
Thomas said to him, "My Lord and my God!"
Then Jesus told him, "Because you have seen me,
you have believed; blessed are those who have not seen
and yet have believed."

John 20:24-29

First of all, Thomas's name means twin in the language the New
Testament is written in, and then many Bible passages include his
Greek nickname—Didymus—which also means twin. We don't really
know why he was nicknamed "twin." Many theologians say he is
probably called this because he had an actual twin, while others say
that he had two dueling personalities. I say both could be true. Maybe
Thomas had an actual twin, but he also had a good self and a bad self,
like so many of us. You know when Homer Simpson from the TV
show *The Simpsons* has that inner battle with himself, symbolized by
an angel on one shoulder and a devil on the other? We all have that
battle, and Thomas, just like us, had a naughty twin, an opposite self.

My naughty twin loves chocolate milkshakes, red meat, and no
exercise. My other self is a vegetarian who avoids sugar and works out
like an athlete. My evil twin always seems to be winning that battle!
(The funny thing is that I'm in Starbucks right now writing this and
sipping on a chocolate Frappuccino. But that's neither here nor there.)

Many of us have a church self and a private self. Some of us are
triplets: We have a church self, a home self, and then a school self.
Some of us might be quintuplets.

The point is, Tom lived a dualistic life, like all of us do. Part of him was willing to die with Jesus, as we read in John 11:16:

> Then Thomas (also known as Didymus) said to the rest of the
> disciples, "Let us also go, that we may die with him."

Thomas was willing to die with Jesus. But he was also the guy who refused to believe in the risen Jesus, even though his friends were pleading with him to believe. This dualism must have been something Jesus saw in Thomas early on. He must have known that Thomas would eventually have to choose which self he would allow to win. Jesus gave him the extra push he needed by honoring Thomas's desire to see Jesus for himself.

Jesus knew that behind Thomas's doubt was the real desire to know truth personally. This is also the case with your generation. You want God to be real, to be active and alive. You want to believe in what actually is. You don't want to settle for easy answers and other people's experiences. You want to see for yourself.

If you think about the Scripture passage from John 20 a little more, this interaction could have gone in another direction and changed Thomas's story in a completely different way. The disciples could have been offended by Tom's doubt and skepticism. They could have rebuked him. Tom could have left thinking, "I'm never coming back here again!" But the environment of the disciples wasn't negative. On top of that, of course, Jesus himself goes above and beyond to honor Thomas's questions. Jesus pursues Thomas and meets him in the midst of all of his doubts. This changes everything for Thomas. And not just for Thomas—this interaction also changed everything for India. Which brings me back to Kerala.

I was speaking about Thomas at an event not long ago and I mentioned the region in India called Kerala, where Thomas established seven churches. Afterward a woman came up and said that she was born and raised there—her home church was one of the seven that Tom planted. Amazing! Absolutely amazing. She said that all of the churches planted by Thomas are still thriving, and the whole region of Kerala is full of committed Jesus followers.

How did this happen? Well, like those of your generation, Thomas wanted more than warm feelings and an experience with Jesus. He definitely wasn't looking for religion. There was a deep longing in Thomas to be part of a movement, and that longing is what woke him up to living out his true identity.

After Jesus's death and resurrection, Thomas ended up traveling all the way down the coast of India telling people about the risen Jesus and how Jesus had profoundly changed him. He kept traveling, looking for open hearts and minds, and finally got to the people of Kerala (where my wife's professor was born). There he found a receptive group, and Tom ended up planting those seven churches to keep up with the great multitudes of new believers. He eventually left that region and had headed into a new area to start an eighth congregation when the leaders of that new area killed him for all of the mess that this new faith was causing.

When we look more closely at the story of Thomas, we see a kid becoming an adult. Right there in the Scriptures we see the adolescent journey taking place as Thomas unloads his childish and small-minded thinking and embraces a robust and category-shattering person by the name of Jesus. He moves from disbelief to belief, then into a full-on movement.

Last week I was with a good friend of mine. This person is from India and is not a believer at all, but is one of my favorite people to hang out with. He's hilarious, irreverent, and incredibly smart. We were talking about India and the community he grew up in when I asked, "Have you ever been to Kerala?"

He looked surprised that I had even had heard of that region. "Oh, that's on my bucket list," he said. "It's one of the best places to go in all of the world."

"Really?" I asked. "Why?"

"Because it's not only a beautiful area, but the people there are known for being some of the most educated and intellectual in all of India."

Imagine that: The place where doubting Thomas planted seven churches is also the region known for being full of Christian intellectuals. What a legacy Thomas has there!

At our youth group's winter camp last year, Kelsey was in a room with a group of tenth grade girls. All of them were talking about how they were sensing God and how they were being challenged in their thinking. One girl, in the midst of all of this faith talk, passionately interjected her frustration. She wasn't experiencing what everyone else seemed to be.

Everyone listened. When she finished talking, my wife looked at her and said, "Oh wow, that is really good—I've been there. Please tell us more about that." Kelsey said it was really something to see this girl explore her questions and slowly calm down and open up a bit. As the weekend went on, my wife saw this girl continue to journey toward something deeper. It wasn't that she hadn't been open to faith, it's that she was, basically, Thomas. Everyone else was experiencing God and she wasn't, and she really wanted to. By the end of that weekend, she took some significant steps toward Jesus. It was her doubt and frustration voiced in a safe community that led her to openness and continued digging.

A couple of years ago I was one of the keynote speakers at a student conference. I was scheduled to speak about the cross on the third night. My goal was to reframe the gospel in a way that helped make sense of the cross within the larger story of faith. I ended my talk by mentioning that the cross of Jesus was the very thing that led people in the first century into a revolution—a movement. I said that this revolution is the very thing God calls us into. The Christian faith is a movement we get to belong to. It changes everything. Jesus is calling us to make some hard decisions and join him.

I was amazed by the response of the teenagers that night. I could really feel them with me. You know those nights where the room is warm with God's palpable presence and everyone is quietly on the edge of their seat? This was one of them.

I was only asked to give one talk at the event, and so I was hoping that the next speaker would do a "now what" talk that next day, continuing the idea of faith as a movement. Instead, he basically got up and talked about having a childlike faith. He spoke against asking questions and doubting. He told us to live sinless lives.

To me what he was actually describing was not a child*like* faith, but a child*ish* faith. There's a big difference. I sat there and was grieved. I felt like these teenagers were dying to know what Christian faith means to the world. I sensed that they, like me, were longing to know how to get in on what God was already doing. That story excites us. It resonates with each one of us. They already knew what *not* to do, but they were dying to know what *to* do.

So I walked up and interrupted the speaker at the end of his talk. I said, "What this guy is saying is not what this whole thing is really about! This is not the story that you've been invited into. It's so much bigger than that!"

No, just kidding. Ha! That would have been a real jerk move. Instead, I sat there, quietly stewing in my frustration.

Afterward, though, I was hanging out in the lobby area when a guy came up to me. "Brock," he said, "I want to know more about the movement thing you mentioned. I'm longing for more and I'm really wanting to know what it looks like to actually follow Jesus in my everyday!"

He was longing for more than an intellectual belief system. He was longing for more than a sin management program. He wanted to be part of something greater than himself. And I don't think he was or is alone in his feelings.

Faith is a movement. Faith is something that empowers and calls you to make a difference in your youth group, in your school, even at home. It's a faith that might even call you to India, asking you to bring with you the best news possible.

*Never pity missionaries; envy them.
They are where the real action is—where
life and death, sin and grace, Heaven and
Hell converge.*

–Robert C. Shannon

8 | BEATNIKS, HIPPIES, AND JESUS FREAKS

When I was about ten years old my dad took a job in a church. Now, I have a confession to make. I hated it. Like, seriously. My dad was a radical and the church seemed to want to tame and sanitize him. For me, the best thing about going to church was leaving.

Eventually, though, I made a group of friends close to my age and we thought of a way to make church adventurous: by sneaking out of the services. Every fifteen seconds one of us would leave the sanctuary in what we thought was a casual way. (I mean, there's no way anyone would ever guess what we were up to, right? So what if eight kids nonchalantly walk out of the church service every fifteen seconds?) We'd get out of there and walk around outside or maybe head into my dad's office.

You may have guessed it by now: We were not very bright. Not at all. Which leads me to the next part of the story. This was in the 1980s, and we were living in the Washington, DC, area. And so what should ten- and eleven-year-olds who are bored at church do, considering that they're just down the road from the White House? I know. Let's prank call it! That sounds like a good idea!

The first time we prank called the White House, we were all laughing so hard. We also wouldn't have been surprised if the FBI had busted down the door to my dad's office and arrested all of us. We felt what I can only describe as a happy terror.

The truth is, church had never really resonated with me, even though I was there all of the time. I never fully understood what we were doing. I didn't really get it. Maybe I'm not that weird, because I've sensed from time to time that I'm not alone in this. Church always has felt to me like a team in the locker room talking about the game plan or maybe a school at a pep rally—but where the team never leaves the locker room and gets on the buses to go to the game and play.

I was born at the beginning of what was known as the Jesus movement in the early 1970s. This movement was a big deal! At the time, thousands upon thousands of teenagers in every city in the country were opening their lives to Jesus. My parents were in a Christian rock band at the time, so for about the first ten years of my life I lived on a tour bus going from town to town, seeing these teenagers join the movement of Jesus. It was genuinely exciting and meaningful—a legitimate revolution.

Maybe you've heard about this Jesus movement. To get a full sense of the larger narrative, you'd have to go back to the 1950s, to the Beatniks, and even before that to the 1940s. (I know—Beatnik. What in the world is that? Well, hold on, this is going to get good!)

America entered World War II just after Pearl Harbor in December of 1941. Hundreds of thousands of young men enlisted in the war and when they left home, the women joined the workforce. This meant that the children of that generation were kind of on their own because there were no real systems in place to care for them. Imagine being a little kid when, all of a sudden, your dad is gone and your mom, for the first time in American history, leaves home to join the workforce.

You and all of the neighborhood kids are left to make it on your own. This doesn't seem like a big deal compared to the culture we live in today, but this was a massive shift in American life for families. Everyone was sacrificing for the cause of freedom.

The war was gruesome and many lives were lost, but evil was slain and in 1945 young men returned home from the war. They did what any of us would do if we were in their shoes: They got together with the wives, who then become pregnant, causing a huge baby boom.

Why I tell you all of this is because something incredible happened five years later, in September of 1950: Millions more children than ever before began their education in kindergarten. In fact, I once heard a speaker at a national youth worker conference put the increase at six million. That's six million more children than the U.S. had ever had enrolled in kindergarten, which happened specifically because of that post-war baby boom. 1950 marked a major transition for schools all over the country. In response to the changes, leaders in education strategized a brand-new way of doing school using the divide and conquer method. American schools moved from one room schoolhouses to grade-specific education.

This is significant because it was the birth of the peer pressure phenomenon. Before 1950, you'd have one teacher and a bunch of different-aged students in one room. The older students wouldn't only work on their own schoolwork, but would help the younger students. In many ways it was a great environment for learning, with the older students being taught how to teach and mentor as well as setting the pace and atmosphere of the classroom. When the new single-age classroom system began, suddenly there was no depth, no student leaders, and only peer influence in each classroom.

So, you have to picture this for a moment. You have these older children who were running the streets while dad was away at war and mom was working. On top of that there are now six million additional kindergartners. The older children and the younger kids all have dads who are home from the war, but many of whom are suffering from PTSD and are struggling to cope. All of this leads to children who are really hurting and feeling lost. People in the older generation noticed that youth and kids seemed aimless, apathetic, and rebellious. (Sound familiar?) Throughout the country, people began to question the practice of age-specific classrooms, but weren't sure of another way forward. Sociologists, reporters, and writers at the time began to call these young people the "beat-down generation."

In and around 1958, thousands of teenagers were taking part in large gatherings across the country, in New York City, in Portland, Oregon, in San Francisco, and many other large cities. A particular young man noticed this and saw that they were wide open for a movement. He was a young Catholic poet and American novelist by the name of Jack Kerouac, who had a heart for the youth of the late '40s and early '50s. He had a vision of rejecting the "beat-down" label the media and sociologists had stuck on this generation. He turned the term on its head by calling them "beatniks," a group led by the spirit of the beatitudes.

Let me pause here for a second. This makes me think again of how people have labeled your generation. *Disengaged. Hurting. Addicted. Self-obsessed. Shallow.* I wonder how we can flip the switch on these labels and provide vision for a new and better way.

Now back to the beatniks and how Kerouac painted a beautiful picture of what could be for these young people. He clarified the cause of this teen movement, and at New York's Hunter College playhouse in 1958, Kerouac said, "It's because I am Beat, that is, I believe in beatitude and that God so loved the world that He gave His only begotten son to it."[14] He went on to describe the beatitudes and how this generation would be known by them.

It's interesting to see Kerouac's impact on the whole beatnik scene. Even his passion for art and poetry had profound influence, as the beatnik generation embraced poetry and all forms of art by gathering in coffeehouses all over the country to read poetry to each other with a bongo player providing background, texture, and mood to the art form. In 1959, the TV show *Dobie Gillis* famously based characters on the beatniks of the day and became the first series where the central characters were all teenagers. The main character's sidekick, Maynard G. Krebs, was a stereotype of how adults viewed the beatnik. All of these sensitive teenagers, who seemed like they were just kind of floating and hanging out together, were also passionate about what was happening in the world.

As the 1960s progressed, disillusionment set in as many leaders of the movement began to die from drug overdoses or simply disappear. Many fell deep into ineffectiveness due to heroin and other hallucinogens or alcohol abuse. Even Kerouac died from the effects of alcoholism. This was all happening in the midst of the angsty teenage beatnik movement.

As these children got older, the beatniks became the hipsters, and the hipsters eventually morphed into the hippies of the mid-1960s. By this time they had forgotten their core reason for existence and embraced a lesser version with free love, drug use, and a vague spirituality. Over time this multi-decade movement—which began with students in the mid- to late-1950s and was forged by youth workers and visionaries like Kerouac who led the way—lost steam. Like many movements, it lost its first love.

But just when one might think the whole thing was a loss, something fortunate happened. A beautiful full circle occurred. In the late 1960s into the early 1970s, teens turned back to the beatitudes with an even more robust embrace of Jesus. In June of 1971, *Time* magazine's cover story, "The Jesus Revolution,"[15] was all about it. What was happening was a phenomenon. Hundreds of thousands of teenagers all over the country were giving their lives to Jesus. What's cool about this story for me is that it was at the beginning of the Jesus movement in 1969 that my parents started a hippie Jesus rock and roll band that lasted through the 1970s.

My parents' band played at the Billy Graham crusades, which were gatherings in huge stadiums where people would hear the gospel in a compelling way. My parents' band was a big draw for teenagers, and we saw thousands of young people come to the Lord. During our time on the road we'd travel into a city and find the highest spot in town. Together we'd look down over the whole of the city and pray that God would do an amazing work there. Every week, multitudes were opening their lives to Christ. As a little guy I was filled with passion over this. But, as I've shared, it ruined me for status quo church living. I just couldn't sit in rows for the rest of my life hearing someone else talk about Christian faith. I wanted to actually live this thing out. This passive approach to faith just seemed irrelevant to me. I couldn't do it then. I've never been able to.

By the time the 1980s hit, the Jesus movement had ended for a variety of reasons, and my parents quit the band to become youth pastors. Like I wrote earlier, going from the tour bus to the church was a difficult transition for me.

I've often wondered, how did I move from being someone who'd sneak out of church and prank call the White House to becoming someone who now works with passionate young people who are opening their lives to Jesus?

When my parents quit the band, I struggled so much. I struggled socially, academically, and even spiritually, with my faith. But then one day in the mid-1980s, when I was in eighth grade, I heard the gospel at youth group in a way that resonated. The way this speaker talked about what it meant to actually follow Jesus reminded me of my childhood. What he described was a movement. He explained that God was on the move and was calling us to join him. I went forward that day and reaffirmed my faith in Jesus, but it didn't take long for me to realize that I hadn't really signed up for a movement. It was more like I'd signed up to sit back down in a row of seats at church and simply talk about faith for the rest of my life. I noticed all of the talk about salvation at my church was focused on the next life. It had nothing to do with *this* current life. On top of all of that, I gathered that I had signed up to no longer have fun. It seemed like Christian faith was all about *not* doing stuff.

When I went forward,
I thought I was signing up for a mission.
I thought I was signing up for a life empowered by God himself.

I thought I was signing up for true community. I thought I was signing up for a life where love, joy, peace, patience, kindness, goodness, and self-control would just bubble out of me. I thought I was joining a cause that would bring those things to others and invite them into a life of meaning and significance.

This is what interested me.

I felt like what I actually received was a bait and switch. I was told that following Jesus was an adventure, but after I asked Christ into my life, I was told to be quiet, to listen and be a good little boy.

Don't get me wrong, I loved hearing about Jesus living life the way it was meant to be lived, and then inviting everyone to join him. In these stories about Jesus, the people actually went places and did things—even scary, uncomfortable things. I loved hearing about that! I was drawn to that.

If you read the stories of Jesus, you'll notice that literally thousands joined him. These people believed, and they followed him at great risk to themselves. Great risk interested me.

It was a struggle then, this following Jesus thing! And man, it's a struggle now, actually following Jesus. Not only with our minds, but with our feet and with our voices.

Listening to many preachers today, though, you wouldn't know that it's hard to actually follow Jesus. They often give the impression that faith is pretty easy and doesn't require much. But what I'm interested in isn't legalism, it's living the way of Jesus and being someone who represents the reign of Christ, extending it everywhere we go.

The reality is that you are made for such movements.

About fifteen years ago I started researching youth movements around the globe. That is when I learned about two great organizations, one called Alpha and one known as the 24-7 Prayer movement in England. These movements are mostly taking place outside of a standard church setting, and are attracting large numbers of young people who are opening their lives to the way of Jesus in the here and now.

I recently took my youth leader team to the church in London that birthed the organization Alpha to see what they are doing. My team came in thinking that faith in Jesus was dead in Europe, which is a common belief, only to discover just the opposite. I talked with a European youth worker there and asked her what was happening in England. Why is the Christian faith exploding in young people there?

She said three things. She said:

It's mostly happening outside of the walls of the church, where kids actually are, in their world.
It's empowered and led by the youth themselves.
It's wide open to the Holy Spirit.

Sounds like the kind of movement I want to be a part of!

We must have a pie. Stress cannot exist in the presence of a pie.

–David Mamet, *Boston Marriage*

9 | ROBBERS, SNOW ANGELS, AND BOLD NEW WAYS

I stood in front of a group in the ski chalet one evening. We were all excited because over the next three days we'd be skiing and snowboarding down Big Bear Mountain. This place contains one of the few SuperPipes in Southern California. A SuperPipe is a twenty-two-foot halfpipe that is beyond epic and ridiculously scary. The excitement in our group was palpable.

That was the feeling in the air as I stood in front of about fifty of our high schoolers for a talk. I asked them a question they weren't expecting: "What is robbing from you?" They looked at me with funny expressions. "Ya know, like, what is stealing your peace, your joy, your freedom?" I asked. "What is taking all of your time and your thoughts? What is stealing from you and giving little in return?"

One guy, Ben, blurted out, in a louder voice than expected, "SCHOOL!" The whole group moaned in unison. Anita spoke up in agreement. "It's like everyone around us— our teachers, our parents, and even our friends—is telling us that if we don't take all of these

AP courses and get ridiculously high GPAs and work on building our resumes that our futures will be ruined." Then Lisa spoke up, almost in a whisper. "Yeah, my parents talk about how fun high school was for them, but the reality is that every one of my friends and person at my school is so stressed. Fun seems to be a rare commodity."

The mood had changed, and there was kind of a pause. All of us sat in the quiet and took a beat, just breathing, almost in unison.

"Is it true?" I asked. Everyone looked at me confused, so I rephrased my question. "Is all of this work and anxiety and worry worth it? Will it pay off?"

Ben, one of our leaders who was now a college student, chimed in. "Nope."

"What? Why?" I asked.

"Brian and I have been talking about all of the stress we felt and work we did in high school and how it made it where we hardly had any time to go to youth group and to bring change to our schools and communities," responded Jeff, another college-aged leader. "It stole all four years from us. Yes, we got into the schools we both wanted to be in, but to be in honest, his school and my school are basically the same thing." Jeff and Brian had realized that some of their online classes at these two different schools were identical—in a sense, working so hard to get into and choose just the right school had ended them at the exact same place, which was disillusioning. "A lot of our classes are online and even though we go to different schools, the classes are literally the same online class. Like, exactly. It's insane!" The atmosphere started getting uncomfortable. Grumblings and side conversations started all over the room.

"Hold on," I said. "Wait up for a minute, gang. We've opened a can of worms here, but let me get us back to the heart of what we are talking about. There's a question I want us to think through over the next few days." I paused before asking, "What gives you life and what is taking life from you? And where is God in all of this?"

Shortly after that we wrapped up our time together, played some board games, ate some fudgie love (brownie batter, minus the egg, that you dip graham crackers into—it's the best ever!) and hung out until bedtime. All of us were excited to get up the next day and hit the slopes for a morning of epic skiing.

> "A thief has only one thing in mind—he wants to steal, slaughter, and destroy. But I have come to give you everything in abundance, more than you expect—life in its fullness until you overflow!"
>
> John 10:10 (TPT)

We hit the mountain early the next morning. I mostly hung out with a group of about six high school students. On one run, we spotted an awesome jump about twenty-five yards ahead. Everyone wanted to take it. I, however, was scared to death. A sixteen-year-old named Jamie was the first to go. I don't think I've ever seen anyone fly that high in my entire life, but his landing didn't go so well. In fact, I've also never seen anyone land that hard. We all gasped in unison as Jamie crashed onto his side and then tumbled, his skis and poles all flying in different directions. "Dang it, that had to hurt!" I said.

As I watched each person fly off this jump—all of them also crashing—I became more and more nervous. I mean, come on, I'm no spring chicken. I'm getting older and older by the minute. I was starting to talk myself out of it when everyone began chanting "Brock! Brock! Brock!" The peer pressure was immense, only these weren't my peers. These were mostly fifteen- and sixteen-year-olds.

I finally got the nerve and headed toward the jump as slowly as anyone has ever approached a jump. But right before I hit it, I caught unexpected speed. I flew through the air—like, unbelievable air. I swear, I flew about ten, maybe fifteen feet, and finished with the most beautiful landing. I'm certain it was the most incredible landing anyone has ever seen in history. I was like a swan in flight. There should have been a camera because it would have made me a YouTube sensation. I screamed, "YES suckers!" But then, out of nowhere, Jamie (in his jealousy and bitterness, of course—ha!) stuck out his ski and tripped me. I crashed, tumbling head over heels to a (fortunately) soft landing. Once everyone saw that I was okay, we all lay there in the snow, laughing our tails off. I'm not sure I've ever laughed that hard. Over time we've retold this story, and with each retelling, the story has gotten bigger and better and more epic. So fun!

We headed the rest of the way down the mountain so we could catch the ski lift for another run. Kari, a seventeen-year-old girl, skied over to ask if she could ride the lift with me. "Of course," I said. "I've been wanting to catch up with you anyways."

We got on the chairlift. "I've been haunted by our conversation last night," she said. "When we all went to bed I started googling and researching this college thing. Brock, I think it's all a lie. It's all about money. And it's killing us!"

"What do you mean?" I asked.

"Well, the College Board, which is supposedly a nonprofit, profited 916 million dollars last year. They also have convinced the government that AP courses are the best way to get students prepared for the SATs. Because of that, the Board made 408 million dollars just from fees for the test and all of the instructional materials. This is crazy!"[16]

"Wow. You researched all of this last night?" I asked.

"Yeah," she said. "You were talking about how even ten or fifteen years ago there wasn't this much pressure to take all of these classes and do all of this prep work. I feel like we've been duped."

I thought about what she was saying. "Well, maybe what started out as something innocent has gotten out of control," I said. "And like so many things that start out to benefit kids, now the adults in charge are lining their own pockets with money."

We sat in thoughtful quiet for a moment, taking in the views of the snowy mountain and the snowboarders below.

Kari had another thought. "You know that I'm one of the top three students in my class. There's a good chance I could be the valedictorian. But research shows that valedictorians do not go on to necessarily do any better in life than other students. In fact this article I was reading showed that really great students tend to have mastered the art of taking exams, but they aren't necessarily good at being out-of-the-box thinkers. Like this one article said, valedictorians aren't likely to be the future's visionaries. They typically settle into the system instead of shaking things up. This is really bugging me. And it's causing me to question the whole thing. What am I giving all of my life to? It's all been about academic success."[17]

I carefully interrupted. "Maybe, but you love school. You enjoy learning."

"Yes, but there's gotta to be more, right?" she asked. "Like, maybe I should be joining the movement of Jesus like you've been talking about. Maybe I've made a god out of a good thing, which is so typical of me. I take a good thing and I make it the greatest thing. I make it into something that it was never intended to be. Maybe my schooling has become something I've been worshiping. To be honest, I'm not happy. I'm riddled with anxiety. And it's not like it's giving me back anything but misery."

We sat in silence the rest of the way up the chairlift. I sensed God in that moment. It was like he was speaking to Kari and taking time with her. She, in that moment, was discovering something super important. God wanted her to catch this. He was actually speaking to her and, on this retreat, was finally getting her attention. We got off of the chairlift, almost falling and tripping each other up in the process. We laughed, moved to the side, and waited for the rest of our clan to join us.

"Maybe the truth is somewhere in the middle, Kari," I said. "Like, maybe you could make school just a good thing again and then elevate some other things that you find more vital." She flashed a quick smile. The rest of the group had finally all arrived. "Last one down the mountain buys hot cocoa!" I yelled to everyone.

I jokingly gave Jamie a shove and we all began the race down the mountain. Boy, it must have been a sight to see. About ten of us were bombing that sucker, yelling *Yee-haw* and yelping all the way down. By the time we got to the bottom I could hardly breathe. And we all laughed our guts off when Jamie came in last. (Of course he said I cheated because of the little "nudge." What the heck?)

We went inside the chalet where I bought everyone drinks and snacks. As we were all hanging out, from time to time I'd catch Kari's eye and smile. We both knew that we were experiencing something real in that moment. True community. It was something she had not had time for because she'd been so busy with school. It was like God was healing her heart from all that she had missed over the past couple of years.

When there was a good time to talk I asked them all a question. "Okay," I said. "How can we make time for this kind of stuff when we get home? What can we cut?" Jamie spoke up. "I can think of an AP course or two." We laughed, finished our cocoa, and headed out for another run.

That wasn't the end of it, though. Over the next few months I watched Kari make some beautiful and inspiring changes, changes that many didn't understand. Changes that were difficult and courageous. She stopped taking a couple of AP courses. She also started a morning prayer walk around her school, and launched a new club at her school focused on intellectual and academic reasons for faith. Really, that club became a little movement. She also started volunteering in our youth ministry, helping plan out-of-the-box ideas that literally brought new life to our community and also brought new people into our group.

Small adjustments can be powerful. When we lean into God's dream for us and the world, new ideas are birthed. New ways are carved out. Good living finally emerges.

Why can't we go backwards...for once?
Backwards, really fast. Fast as we can.
Heh heh. Really put the pedal to the metal,
you know? Bill and Ted did it.

–Halliday, *Ready Player One*

10 | BROKEN-DOWN WALLS

"Brock, I have to talk to you. Right now!" We were at youth group when this high schooler pulled me around the corner, away from the crowd of teens and leaders. "I keep messing up!" she said. "I start to feel stress or anxiety and I can't keep myself from falling back into my old habits! I just made my New Year's resolutions. Two of my goals were to start sharing my faith with my friends and to read the Bible more, and move away from all of the crap. But I have zero self-control. There's something wrong with me!"

I remember having similar thoughts. When I was in eighth grade I was struggling. Struggling quite a bit, in fact. Who isn't in eighth grade, right? In some sense, it was actually good for me. In eighth grade I was becoming very aware of my own brokenness. I was becoming aware of my own inclination toward sin. When you're younger you believe that you'd never do certain things or cross certain lines. It's a pretty naive thing to think, but it's very common. Here's why: At that point, you don't realize that not doing certain things requires extreme discipline. It means we have to know ourselves and make plans for ourselves. Do you want to know why I've never done cocaine? Well, here's my answer: Because, based on what I know about it, I know I'd like it. I know that when people try certain drugs they end up really enjoying them. It would be extremely naive for me to think that I'm above liking something that is really bad for me. And so, to keep myself safe and healthy, I avoid it altogether.

Anyway, back to me being in eighth grade. I was making subtle compromises in my life, and they were starting to affect my everyday. I was wondering things like, "What's the big deal about getting drunk anyway?" In reality I had no access to alcohol, so making an actual decision about alcohol didn't get played out in my life at that point. But the thing is, it all begins in the mind. Everything starts from a thought. A simple, sometimes compromising, thought.

For me, it began with girls. In eighth grade, girls were starting to pay attention to me for the first time. And let's just say that I was liking it. To be honest, girls began to consume my mind. And then it was affecting some of my actions.

For the first time I had interactions with girls who liked me. Like with any temptation, what started out as kind of cool and fun slowly and very subtly led me into shallowness and compromise. It was barely perceptible at first, but obsessing over girls did not feed my soul; in fact, it led to deeper longing. Something was missing. I felt hollow and empty, and I was moving more and more toward spiritual apathy. I didn't like how I was feeling at all.

One night at youth group I was sitting in my normal spot in the back row, hanging with my friends. But you know those moments when it feels like the speaker is speaking directly to you? That night I had one of them. When the speaker talked about knowing Jesus and following Jesus, I blinked back tears. My emotions overwhelmed me. It truly surprised me and I tried to get my composure so my friends wouldn't notice. My brain was yelling, "Brock, get ahold of yourself, man!" But in that moment, I became very aware of my need. I needed God to work in my life in a very real way. The shallow fulfillment of the world was pulling me further and further away from him, and I had been letting it happen. In fact, I had no strength at all. My numbness and apathy were exhausting me. I had zero self-control and my hang-ups were beginning to own me.

One of my favorite proverbs is from chapter 25. Here it is:

> A person without self-control
> is like a city with broken-down walls.
>
> Proverbs 25:28 (NLT)

I was like a city with broken-down walls. In fact, I was like a city with no walls at all. All seemed well as long as the enemy wasn't coming, when things were easy. But when temptation came running after me and apathy was pressing in, I had no protection. It's funny. All is good and peaceful for a city without walls—that is, unless the enemy is storming the castle. All is good unless a battle is underway. It was in eighth grade that I finally became aware that a battle was happening within me and I had zero protection. I had very little strength. I had no walls and so I was so susceptible to attack from all sides.

Listening to this speaker, I felt myself waking up to the power and presence of God. I knew something needed to change. I was recognizing things I hadn't known even a few moments prior. Fortunately, this speaker invited us up to the front to get prayed for and I ran up there. I literally ran. At that point I didn't care what my friends were going to do. The speaker prayed for me, saying, "God, fill this young man with your Spirit. Empower him. Strengthen him." When he said these words, something happened that to this day is hard for me to explain. It was like a power flowed through my body. If this has happened to you, then you know what I'm talking about. If you've never experienced this, though, it might sound strange or made up. It was like electricity was flowing through me. Not shocking electricity, but a warm power that started at the top of my head and moved through my body, all the way down my spine to the bottoms of my feet. I wasn't sure what was happening, but it was accompanied with an overwhelming sense that this power flowing through me was God, with this unfathomable peace and joy and freedom. Later I would discover that in actuality this was God's Spirit working in me, getting my attention. Possibly starting the process of renovating my broken-down walls.

Here's the thing. The Christian faith is weird. I am the first to admit that. And I am not one to "just believe" things. I believe that scientists do great work and their research should be heeded. Rational thought should be practiced in most decision-making processes. A great many things have explanations. But then, a great many things do not have explanations. And this is one of those mysteries, as explained in I Corinthians 6:19-20:

> Do you not know that your bodies are temples of the Holy Spirit, who is in you, whom you have received from God? You are not your own; you were bought at a price. Therefore honor God with your bodies.

I had been living my life without a sense of God's Spirit working. In fact, I was almost completely ignoring God. I did believe in Jesus, but there wasn't any sense of actually following him, being used by him, being strengthened in him, and living a life dependent on him. I wasn't living in a way where I was actually open to, or even aware of, his Spirit giving me what I needed to live life freely and fully. I was just pretty much thinking about girls. Okay, not totally true. I was thinking about girls and sports. Can't forget sports. Nothing really wrong with that, except that I was living like the Corinthian church from that Scripture you just read. I was ignorant of the fact that there was a power present inside my life, inside of my body. I didn't know that I was a temple of the Holy Spirit. I didn't know that I was the dwelling place of God's Spirit. I didn't know that I was supposed to, on the regular, allow God's Spirit to empower me. Which brings me to another passage:

> Do not get drunk on wine, which leads to debauchery. Instead, be filled with the Spirit, speaking to one another with psalms, hymns, and songs from the Spirit. Sing and make music from your heart to the Lord, always giving thanks to God the Father for everything, in the name of our Lord Jesus Christ.
> Ephesians 5:18-20

This passage is pretty darn cool. We can fill ourselves with so many things. We can fill up our time and lives with gaming, with romance, with drugs and alcohol. You name it, we can find some way to make it a priority and give it power in our lives. But this passage is challenging us. All of that other stuff is empty and won't lead us into life. Ephesians is calling us to take the time to be empowered by God's Spirit.

Have you ever wondered what is the evidence of God's Spirit working in you? Well, the writers of the New Testament called it fruit. The "fruit" was the tangible evidence, like fruit on a tree, that God's Spirit had taken up residence in you.

> But the fruit of the Spirit is love, joy, peace, forbearance, kindness, goodness, faithfulness, gentleness and self-control. Against such things there is no law.
> Galatians 5:22-23

Wow. These are all things that I need in my life, but at that point in eighth grade that last one really hit home: self-control. A person with self-control is like a city with strong walls. I needed some walls, man!

After getting prayed for I didn't want to go back to my seat. I just stood at the front of this room. I had been prayed for before. I had sensed God before. But for whatever reason, this time I was ready for something beyond an experience. I really was dying for a life worth living, and I knew the stuff I had slowly been getting into was robbing from me. I was tired of one-off experiences with God that made little difference in my life the next day. You know, you go to a camp and you start living for Jesus and experiencing authentic community and your life is overflowing with joy and peace and all of that good fruit. But a week after camp the glow starts to fade. Why? Because you've stopped living the way you were living at camp. You've stopped allowing God's Spirit to work daily in your life.

If we are going to start a movement, then we are going to need a power that is beyond us. We know ourselves. We know that we are capable of all sorts of junk. Junk that robs us, steals from us, and destroys us.

It leaves us robbed of love.
Robbed of peace.
Robbed of forbearance (this word actually means tolerance).
Robbed of kindness.
Robbed of faithfulness.
Robbed of gentleness.
Robbed of self-control.

The apostle Paul, who gave us this Scripture in Galatians 5, was writing to people who were struggling. They were under so much persecution, feeling so much discord and confusion, that they were desperate. Desperate for the very same things we need today. And unlike comic book heroes who covet supernatural abilities to punch, fly, and psychically manipulate others, these superpowers give us the ability to love God, love others, and live remarkable lives. Punching your way out of difficulty or manipulating world leaders into doing the right things is not the way of Jesus. Besides, our own worst enemy is often ourselves. Jesus is love and we, all of us, have choices in this life. I choose to live like a city of refuge on a hill, lights blazing. A city that has built-up walls of character. I choose to live with the ability to say "No" to myself and "Yes" to God. And I get to lead others out of the emptiness and into the fullness of that same kind of life.

Oh, I love those passages in Galatians and Ephesians. Go check them out and highlight some of the parts that jump out to you. Ephesians 5 and Galatians 5. Those are words that could help us start a movement!

Jesus is not respectable or nice in the sense of being placid or uncontroversial. He is not necessarily a good citizen. Jesus is wildly and prophetically subversive, [and...] not all is right. And something has to change.

–Craig Greenfield, *Subversive Jesus: An Adventure in Justice, Mercy, and Faithfulness in a Broken World*

11 | THE SUBVERSIVE GOSPEL

It had been another ordinary night at youth group, but my hope and prayer was that God would make it extraordinary. I had, once again, called our youth into the movement that is the Christian faith, but was not sure if the message had hit its mark. So I was pleased when two of our guys walked up to the front and, after introductory fist bumps, got really serious.

"Brock, we have to get with you soon," said Clay. Tommy nodded his head in agreement. "Sure, what's up?" I asked, thrilled that these guys obviously cared about the talk tonight. They explained. "We are super confused about what the gospel is after that message. We were talking and I don't think either one of us really understands."

Wow. Surprised, I responded in my best practiced, calm voice. "I was hoping that it would be more clear, not cause more confusion," I said. "Ugh. I'm so sorry. Let's get together soon and talk it through."

A few days later we met at a local coffee shop called Northside Social.

It's become a favorite place for me to work and talk with people. I love the atmosphere, with its old bones that have been dressed up and renovated in a way that makes it appeal to pretty much everyone. The food's pretty good, I love the coffee, and there are spots in the old building where you can have some privacy if you need it. The guys met me with their drinks and we headed upstairs. It was only the three of us in the attic-like space. Clay slid onto the bench and Tommy took the chair next to mine.

After exchanging pleasantries about school and work, they got right into it. "So Brock, I was reading that passage in Romans that you spoke out of again and it's amazing! I think I'm starting to get it," Clay said. I smiled. "Cool, let's look at it together," I said. We opened the Bible apps on our phones to Romans 8:19-21. Tommy read the passage out loud to us:

> For the creation waits in eager expectation for the children of God to be revealed. For the creation was subjected to frustration, not by its own choice,
> but by the will of the one who subjected it...

Tommy stopped reading and took a breath. "This just means that things are screwed up, right?" he asked. I nodded. "Yep." He continued with verse 21:

> ...in hope that the creation itself will be liberated from its bondage to decay and brought into the freedom and glory of the children of God.

"So yes, the world is messed up," I said. "Life is hard, things aren't the way that they are supposed to be, but—and here is the big but—creation is sitting there and waiting. Waiting for something new, waiting for something to change. Creation is expectant. You might think of it like your mom waiting for you to be born. You might not get this at your age but trust me, she was eagerly expecting your birth, meeting you in the flesh. She longed for you to be a reality outside of her body. But in the meantime she was full of a growing baby, a new life. This new life is not just an idea, but a coming reality. She knew that she would give birth in due time."

"The fullness of the gospel is not just about what Jesus did on the cross," I went on. "It is the story of incredible love that has revealed itself to us slowly through time. Like a pregnancy, the people waited for the time when something new would be birthed. Ancient peoples practiced their religions, made their sacrifices, longed for hope. So when Jesus showed up it was clear that he was all about doing something new, totally unexpected."

Clay let out a "Hmmmmm."

"Questions?" I asked.

"Yeah, but can we not talk about birthing stuff anymore? Gross," he said. We could not help but laugh. "But seriously," he continued, "what new things did Jesus bring to the table? I get that he brought new stuff to Israel maybe, but what about to everyone else?"

I thought for a moment before I answered. "You cannot take a story completely out of its context," I said. "You know, the circumstances always inform the setting for what took place. But this story also transcends its own context and has impacted millions of people around the world for over two thousand years. Let's see if I can give you a few things that were surprising or new. For example, Jesus was always saying and doing things that caused problems for people in power at the time. He called the religious leaders a brood of vipers. He healed people on the wrong day of the week, if you can believe there is a right and wrong day for that. He said that the first will be last and the last will be first. The people wanted a leader who would throw down and kill the evil Romans, but Jesus did not do what they wanted. He gave himself over, asking the Father to forgive those who beat him, spit on him, and shouted 'Crucify!' Mostly, he practiced the things he preached. He was there to free people, people who wanted to be freed and restored. But he didn't do it in the way the people thought he should. He was a cultural anomaly. Unexpected, but absolutely expected. Needed. This is a story that resonates—I mean, aren't almost all young adult novels about this?"

"Yeah, that's really true. I loved the Hunger Games series back in middle school. Katniss is totally the unexpected hero," Tommy offered. "Those themes are everywhere."

"Harry Potter!!" exclaimed Clay. We all chuckled at the forcefulness of his words. It was the proverbial light bulb moment for Clay.

"Yeah, Harry Potter is heavy with that same story line," I agreed.

Clay spoke again. "So, there really is, somewhere in the back of our minds, this idea that we need to be freed or rescued or whatever. I don't think I ever noticed that." I could tell by looking at Clay that the wheels of his brain had started turning. He smiled. "Okay," he said. "So that's what you were talking about when you said the gospel is about a rebellion. Jesus did not fit everyone's expectations, and then he was killed for that."

"Yes, and the story doesn't end there," I said. "He passed the baton to us. Jesus told his disciples that they would do even greater things than he did. He equipped them, empowered them, to continue the work of sharing the good news in the world. And the same goes for us—we have been given a commission, like the one military officers get. We have been told to go and tell everyone what we know, to invest in the lives of others, to pray and keep in relationship with God so we can know what's next."

The guys were silent for a minute. "Soooo," Tommy started slowly, "everything and everyone is waiting for God's children to lead us into a rebellion so they can be freed."

"Dude! YES!" I responded. "We all know that the culture is in rebellion away from God, but the whole earth is waiting for a different kind of rebellion, a rebellion that will mean liberation for the whole earth and everything in it. And this rebellion began with Jesus on the cross, when he took in all of our sin; he absorbed all of our anger and disharmony. He then exploded this rebellion, this new way of being alive, into the world at the resurrection. He overcame death and all our junk. And, here's the kicker: Then, he empowered us in this rebellion with his indwelling Spirit. He made a supernatural way for us to overcome evil in our daily lives so we can be difference-makers. Is this making sense?" I asked.

"Yeah, let me take a shot," Tommy said. "Jesus started this rebellion at the cross. He was the ultimate rebel leader." We all started laughing as Clay did his best seated imitation of Darth Vader with a light saber. Tommy continued. "Jesus caused this rebellion to break out into the world at the resurrection, and he's making sure it's still happening by giving us his Spirit to strengthen us."

Clay interjected. "Yeah, it's like he armed that rebellion. He empowered it with his Spirit."

"What were you guys talking about, saying you didn't understand my talk the other night? You two totally get this!" I said.

"Well, we've had time to think it through a bit," Tommy said. "I've always thought that being a Christian was about being a good person."

"Exactly," Clay said. "I mean, yes, Christians are good people, but so are other people. What seems to separate us is that we are called to the frontlines. Because the world is desperate for God's children to be revealed and to actually do something."

"You know," I said, "when the early followers of Jesus called him the Son of God and called him Lord, it was an act of rebellion. Literally, it was a rebellion against the empire. Romans called Caesar the Son of God and they said that he was Lord. So calling Jesus those things was treason. Rome had a full-on rebellion on its hands with these Jesus followers, which they were trying to stop. But they couldn't. No matter what, they couldn't stop this thing."

"So that's what you meant when you said that the gospel is subversive?" Clay asked.

"Yes!" I said. "But it's not just about Rome back in the day. Jesus calls us to see what is evil, what is hurting the poor and marginalized, and do something about it. He is also calling us to buck the systems that keep us subjected to frustration, the ways that lead to death. Today when you say Jesus is in charge, that he is your King, he's your Lord, you are directly defying our current culture. That is, if you live like what you are saying is true. This is the first step. We all have something that masters us and defines us. When you say that Jesus is your master, it defines who you are, who you live for, why you do what you do. It's a big deal."

I paused. "Look at Philippians with me for a second," I said. We each scrolled through our Bible apps to Philippians 2. I read Philippians 2:9-11 out loud.

> Therefore God exalted him to the highest place
> and gave him the name that is above every name,
> that at the name of Jesus every knee should bow,
> in heaven and on earth and under the earth,
> and every tongue acknowledge that Jesus Christ is Lord,
> to the glory of God the Father.

"When Paul wrote this in 50-something A.D. it was an act of rebellion. These words would get you killed," I said, before turning the conversation back toward them. "So what are the things that are dictating your life? What's really leading you?"

Tommy smiled. "Uh, girls."

"Ha! Yes," I said with a laugh.

Clay took in a thoughtful breath and paused. We both looked at him, waiting. Tentatively he asked, "Could fear dictate your life?"

"Of course it could, Clay. Lots of us struggle with fears," I said.

He had a slight frown; it was obvious his mood had shifted. He spoke slowly and precisely. "This movement will only begin when our generation finally says that school and grades and sports are no longer going to dictate every aspect of our lives. I feel so much pressure to be a success, but I don't even know what that really means.

I have to rebel against the things I am afraid of. Saying that Jesus is Lord means that, well, all that stuff can't be so important."

"And girls, don't forget girls, Clay," Tommy said, making us all laugh again.

I swirled the last dregs of my cappuccino around the bottom of my mug. "It's not just that we say no to the things that exert authority over our lives. It's that we wake up to Jesus. We become aware that God's Spirit lives in us and we want to become in tune with that. We let him be in charge. And we don't just say words and read books about it. Those things are important, but following Jesus actually means moving," I said.

"See, there are a couple of kingdoms. There's the kingdom of this world, and we all know the direction that thing is going. It ain't working. Then there's the kingdom of God. This is the kingdom that leads to life," I said.

"But let me talk about the subversive gospel of God's kingdom for a second. The kingdom of God changes everything in your life. Everything is impacted in this kingdom. The way you view yourself. How you see your future. Whether you fill your life up with anxiety or peace. What choices you make online with your phone. Everything contributes to death or to life. God's kingdom is all about living life to the fullest. The other kingdom is in front of our faces every day. It seems alright, but I know your stories, guys. I know the stories of your friends. Those stories are leading you into misery."

"When we give our lives totally and completely to the kingdom of God, what we're doing is based first and foremost in love: God's love for us and, through his empowerment, our love for others. And although it's based in love, it is not safe. We are in the land of epic adventure and high calling. This is a place of transformation, where people are unbelievably changed in their minds and hearts." I paused. "I truly believe what I am about to say to you guys, so listen up. I believe that God has set you two up in his kingdom to do great things." I stopped talking and took it all in.

"Okay, I've got to say something, Brock," Tommy said after the pause. "That's what I really want! I really want to be led by Christ. I'm tired of pretending. I really want Jesus to be my Lord. I'm so ready for this! I don't want to be just a good guy. I want to be someone God is going to use to make a difference."

"Brock, honestly, this is why we wanted to meet with you," Clay said. "We wanted to tell you that we're in! We're ready!"

What I thought was an ordinary night at youth group had turned out to be part of something extraordinary. When Clay and Tommy got up to go, I sat there beyond excited. I honestly could have gotten up right then and there and run a marathon.

Okay, maybe not a marathon, but I could have run a block. Like, a good block.

Our greatest fear should not be of failure but of succeeding at things in life that don't really matter.

–Francis Chan, Crazy Love: Overwhelmed by a Relentless God

12 | BIG NOSE

So, I was born with a fairly large nose, and as I got older I became more and more aware of it. People calling me "beak boy" or asking me to move to the side because my nose was blocking their sun, those were things that clued me in to the fact that I might have an extra-large snout. Like, "Hey Brock, how's it feel to wake up in the morning and smell the coffee… in Brazil?" Yes, I get it, I must have an incredible smeller. I remember asking my mom if I'd ever grow into my nose. Let's just say that I was very aware of it.

One summer around seventh grade my parents sent me to a camp just outside of New York City. Initially I didn't want to go, but when I arrived, it felt like coming home. There were Italians and Greeks all over the place. There were more big noses at camp than at a Big Bird convention. "Yes! I've finally found my people!" I thought. I immediately started growing in confidence. I felt at ease. I didn't at all mind if people could see my profile. I felt normal and it was liberating.

One afternoon at camp I got up the courage to walk over and talk to this girl named Camille. She was really cute and had a lot of friends. Back home I would never talk to a girl like this but, remember, here I was feeling confident and really good about myself. I was with my people, after all. I walked up and starting talking, and she giggled at what I was saying. The conversation was so natural and comfortable. We were hitting it off big time!

But then, something happened that shattered my confidence. All of the sudden I heard a loud voice. In a thick Brooklyn accent some guy yelled, "Hey, big ears!" I ignored it. They couldn't be talking to me. "Yo, big ears!"

After a couple more "big ears" I finally looked over at this guy. "Yeah you, Dumbo!" he said, looking directly at me. "Me?" I asked. "Yeah, you, big ears," he said. I looked at this girl in utter disbelief and asked, "I have big ears too?" Ugh!

Just when I thought I fit in. Just when I thought I didn't stick out like a sore thumb. Oh boy!

When I was in about fifth grade I was walking around the mall with my dad, who was and still is my hero. As we made our way through the mall there were mirrors everywhere. After we had passed by a few of them I realized something: I was like his mini me. I had his face and, not only that, my mom cut our hair the same way. We were even kind of dressed alike. Even though my dad was my hero, I immediately became embarrassed. Honestly, I couldn't get far enough away from him. I went home and asked him to shave my hair and cut lines along the side of my head (total '80s style). I wanted to differentiate myself from him and it couldn't happen soon enough.

My whole life people have said, "Wow, you look like your father!" and "Man, Brock, you are the spitting image of your dad." I'm not sure why, but it kind of embarrassed me. But then one day, when I was in about eighth grade, my friends and I were hanging out in the basement when my dad walked in and started cracking jokes. My friends were on the floor laughing. After he left the room, they looked at me and said, "Brock, you are so lucky! Your dad is the absolute best!" *"What?"* I thought. That moment was surprising for me. Something in my thinking shifted.

In tenth grade I was invited to play at a five-star summer basketball camp. All kinds of famous coaches were there and all of these outstanding players were vying for attention, hoping a scout or a school would notice us. I was a Christian kid but, especially in that setting, I wasn't going to reveal that to anyone. In that environment, surrounded by top high school basketball players from all over the country, I definitely didn't want people to know that I was associated with Jesus.

One afternoon during the camp, though, a few of us were sitting at a table talking when one of the guys mentioned how one time he had accidentally farted during his pastor's sermon and how embarrassing it was. We all laughed at the ridiculousness of the whole thing. But in that moment something else shifted in me. A couple of the other guys started talking about how they went to church, and they didn't seem embarrassed about it at all. What was wrong with me? First I don't want people to know that my dad is my dad, and now I don't want people to know that my Heavenly Father is my Heavenly Father? What the heck?!

A few months later we were at youth group and my dad, who was also our youth pastor, was up front talking about our Heavenly Father and how much he loves us. He was saying how, in Zephaniah 3, God literally sings over us. He loves being our Father and he's so proud of each one of us.

I sat there, astounded. "I really think God is amazing!" a friend of mine said in our small group afterward. "He's everything I ever hoped he'd be!" In that moment, I knew I was the one with the problem. I knew that my thinking had been all wrong. Again, what the heck?! If my Heavenly Father is proud of me, the big-nosed, big-eared, messed-up me, why am I not super proud of being his son? Why am I embarrassed when people notice that I look like him?

All those years ago when Jesus showed up on the scene, he was proud to be his father's son. He told people things like, "When you look at me, it's just like looking at the father" and "my father and I are one" and "whatever my father tells me to do, I do." When people saw Jesus, they knew they were looking at the face of God.

There's this great passage of Scripture in 1 John:

> The Father has loved us so much that we are called children of God. And we really are his children. The reason the people in the world do not know us is that they have not known him.
>
> 1 John 3:1 (NCV)

Like Jesus, we are literally the representation of our Heavenly Father to those around us. When people see you, you remind them of the God who desperately loves them and enjoys them. Your presence in the room with them points them to your Father. This is how we thrive, when we fully embrace who we *really* are. We are God's kids, and as his kids, we have a spectacular calling. When we live out this calling as the children of God, we will live fulfilled lives. We will be who we truly are, unashamed. Not embarrassed. Not even a little. I imagine how my interactions would play out if I approached life this way.

"Man, Brock, you look just like your father."

"Ahhh. Thank you."

*I firmly believe that any man's finest hour,
the greatest fulfillment of all that he holds
dear, is that moment when he has worked
his heart out in a good cause and lies
exhausted on the field of battle—victorious.*

–Vince Lombardi

13 | SUFFERING AS A WAY FORWARD
PART UNO

There this high schooler stood in front of the whole church on a Sunday morning telling his story, about how at our high school houseboats camp, he had discovered Jesus in a life-changing, profound kind of way. There wasn't a dry eye in the place. I sat in the front row with tears in my eyes, listening to this teenager as he described how God had delivered him from addiction. I listened as he said he would never be the same again. Down deep, I knew the struggle in his life was far from over, but I also had hope.

Around this time, our youth ministry took most of the month of August off in order to catch our breath, rest, and gear up for the busy fall months, and by the time our fall kick-off happened this same guy who'd shared about his life in front of our church was conspicuously missing. He was the kind of person who never missed. I called him later that week and left a message. This went on for a number of weeks, him not showing up and me reaching out, with me hearing nothing in response. Finally, he reluctantly agreed to meet me for coffee. After a few minutes of small talk I was bursting inside.

"Dude, what's going on?!" I asked him.

He looked down. "Brock, I just don't believe anymore," he said. I asked him to tell me more.

"I don't know," he said. "I got back from houseboats camp only to fall back into my old habits and addictions and it led me down a dark path. I started really looking at the world and seeing all of the horrible things out there. I have to think that if I were God I wouldn't let all of this stuff continue. I just can't believe anymore."

I understood. I had been there myself. But here's the other thing: I felt guilty, because I felt down deep that I had set this teenager up for failure. This was a person who'd been primed for a movement, but I hadn't readied him for the days and weeks and months ahead. I gave him an easy gospel but I didn't talk about what came next.

There was a period in my own life when I questioned what I'd learned about God. Most of us go through times where we doubt what we've been taught, what we believe, and if it still holds water in the ever-changing world. When I went through this very dark period in my life, it led me to some questions:

God, where the heck are you?
Why do you let bad things happen, especially to innocent people?
Is Christian faith even true?
Can I really trust the Scriptures?

During that time, these kinds of questions flooded my heart and mind. It's remarkable how hard stuff can shake us, how it can cause us to question everything about God. Looking back at the gospel messages I heard growing up, the main lesson I'd taken away was that once I became a Christian, God would protect me, bless me, and bestow me with happiness for all time. I don't think I'm the exception. I think what I heard is very much the norm, especially here in the United States. Somehow the American Dream and Christian faith got blended together in a way that messes everything up.

We have absorbed this kind of thinking, and we've picked up the idea that it's wrong to wrestle with some of the tougher questions. But the number one reason people leave Christianity is because of difficult things—because of their own suffering and the suffering of the world.[13, 14]

Hard things come to us all and, sadly, church doesn't seem to prepare us for them. In fact, the gospel preached at many churches today seems to be very different from the gospel the early church taught. It diverges so much that it would be unrecognizable to the writers of the Scriptures. If we spoke like the early followers of Jesus, we would encourage each other to embrace suffering for the cause of Jesus, not avoid it. The early followers of Jesus somehow believed that it was the difficult things that would produce the best things in our lives. Take a look at Romans 5:3-5:

> Not only so, but we also glory in our sufferings, because we know that suffering produces perseverance; perseverance, character; and character, hope. And hope does not put us to shame, because God's love has been poured out into our hearts through the Holy Spirit, who has been given to us.

That's quite a line there, "...we also glory in our sufferings." The early church really believed this! To me, this is so challenging. What did they know that I don't?

When you look at the confusing and difficult world your generation is trying to navigate, you see that suffering is a part of every teenager's life. Heck, it's part of life no matter what age you are. But if you're not ready for it, a loss of faith is likely waiting for you. If you don't hang in there with God through all the hard stuff, you may never get to that hope on the other side, the hope that is promised to never disappoint. It's too easy to bail before the good stuff emerges. But I get it, it's hard to see that when you're in deep.

I began a habit about fifteen years ago of reading at least one book a year from an atheist (confident God does not exist) or agnostic (unsure about God's existence), or from someone thoughtful outside of the Christian faith. I find that it keeps me on my toes, gets me thinking, and it humbles me. One year I picked up Bart Ehrman's book, *God's Problem*. I was so struck by his story. Ehrman is kind of the poster child for agnosticism and he's a religious studies professor at the University of North Carolina Chapel Hill. In another of his books, *Misquoting Jesus*, he writes about how as a teenager he was convinced that the Christian faith was completely true and that every word of the Bible was divinely inspired. He was completely certain.

I love the Christian writer Anne Lamott's view on this: "The opposite of faith is not doubt, it's certainty."[20] It's funny and resonant, because I have found that my most certain youth group kids are the ones who end up struggling with faith the most during their college and young adult years. Certainty keeps us from asking questions. Certainty keeps us from digging deeper. It keeps us shallow. It's the opposite of faith.

Ehrman became a Christian as a teenager and then went to Wheaton College (a famous Christian college). He felt like God was calling him into ministry, and so went on to Princeton to get advanced degrees in theology. But he writes about how the more he studied, the more he began to question Christian faith altogether. By the time he was approaching his forties he had completely left the faith and embraced agnosticism and a soft atheism.

(I say soft because his wife is still a believer, and this no doubt has an impact on his respect for faith. My wife and I are currently remodeling our home. At this point in our twenty-four-year marriage, I'm wide open to whatever she wants. I've learned this the hard way. In my mind, I can picture Bart and his wife's dinner conversations about faith and it makes me laugh. He says something like, "Honey, faith is ridiculous and I don't get how anyone could believe this... Uhhhmmmm, I mean, you are really wise and smart, so I get why you would think like that..." Ha! Bart, just smile and nod your head.)

What sent Ehrman over the edge, away from faith, was that he wasn't sure what to do with all of the suffering in the world. Again, this is the number one reason young people leave the faith. It is a major player in what is keeping them from the movement. They look at the world and they see all of the brokenness, the pain and tragedy, and they cannot figure out how a loving God would allow or, worse yet, *cause* all of that suffering. I use the word *cause* in response to what many teenagers hear over and over again at church. When someone is suffering they often hear in response the disgusting pat answers of Christian people: "It's all part of God's plan" and "there is a reason for everything" and "God doesn't allow anything you can't handle" and other confusing mumbo jumbo. Hearing this, teenagers wonder, "*Really*? God's plan is that that little girl got abducted and forced into prostitution? *That* is God's plan?"

Even the softer version, the belief that "God allows these things" can be a rough one to work through. It is these easy answers and a theology of certainty that cause so many of our teenagers to struggle. They can lead so many into discouragement, confusion, and, for some, the full abandonment of faith.

I see Ehrman's journey this way:

Doubt ⟶ Faith ⟶ Certainty ⟶ Loss of faith

I find it very interesting that the step right after certainty is a loss of faith. I mentioned how I worry most about the youth who do not seem to have any questions about faith, God, or the universe. With them I try to instigate some sort of doubt. I try to rattle their certainty, not because I want to rattle them, but because I believe it helps introduce them to the mystery that is God. Embracing the questions feeds our wonder. Questions lead us into deeper waters and, ultimately, into more mystery. And mystery is where faith thrives.

Recently I received a letter from a current college student who was in my youth group a couple of years ago. Everyone was always worried about him because he struggled a lot. He was a natural questioner, and simplistic answers never helped him at all. On top of that, his family life was difficult and in eleventh grade his parents got a divorce. This sent him into a pretty dark season. During his high school years I'd reach out to him and we'd get together. He asked me the absolute best questions.

"Brock, we prayed that God would help my parents' marriage come together. Why didn't he answer our prayers?"

"Where is God right now? My home is a wreck and it's getting worse."

"What kind of God would allow such awful things to occur in the world?"

We would sit together, he'd ask questions, and I'd quietly listen and offer what wisdom I could. I talked to him about how God had given us, as his children, an immense gift called choice. We get to choose what kind of life we want: a life with him, or a life separate from him. Some people use this choice for good, others for selfish reasons.

That would help him a bit, but it also would open up more questions. When you ask questions with a humble and tender heart, good things can happen.

I see it this way:

Doubt —→ Mystery —→ Faith

Back to the letter he wrote me from college. This is part of what he said: "Brock, thank you for sitting with me in my questions and in my pain. You never gave up on me and you never offered me easy answers. You just listened. You walked with me through all of this and then you ultimately pointed me to the God who is with me. With me in the midst of all of the hard stuff. I'm just grateful! You helped me beyond my doubts to a faith full of mystery and wonder. And I like that!"

I wonder what storms you're going through right now? I wonder what tragedy is overwhelming you at this point in your life? I wonder if you have thought about one of the greatest mysteries in life, one that so many others have contemplated? This mystery is something that we'll look at in the upcoming chapters: that God's name is Immanuel, God with us.

Thomas, nicknamed the Twin, said to his fellow disciples,
"Let's go, too—and die with Jesus."

–John 11:16 (NLT)

14 | SUFFERING AS A WAY FORWARD
PART DOS

What's fascinating to look at is how the writers of the New Testament, and the early church followers of Jesus, understood suffering. They knew they lived in a broken world and that people suffered because of it. They also knew that there was an enemy who played a major role in the world. In the midst of all of that they still chose to follow Jesus, knowing full well that it would naturally lead them into extreme hardship. These New Testament writers were so convinced of God's love that they believed God would work things out for their good in the end, despite the evil intentions of the enemy or of other human beings. He would take all of the horror in the world and make it right one day. Did they fully understand any of this? No. But they were okay living in the tension of it all. They embraced mystery. They didn't feel the need to have all of their questions answered.

If you look back at Peter's story in the Scriptures, you'll find that he denied knowing Jesus to avoid suffering. But later he recognized that an embrace of suffering is what could actually lead him, and others, into a deeper faith. In fact, at Peter's reinstatement, not long after Jesus's resurrection and appearance on the beach, Jesus tells Peter that if he joins the movement, one day Rome will stretch his hands and lead him where he does not want to go; they will kill him, like Jesus (John 21:18-19). Then Jesus says, "Follow me." That's not an easy gospel. Ha! I can imagine how this would go over at my next youth camp. "Everybody, come forward if you want to follow Jesus. But know this! If you follow him, it will lead to suffering and probably your death. Come on down, people!"

Eventually, Peter starts to look at suffering differently. He begins to call people to join in the movement, even knowing the cost. Rather than explain it away, dismiss it, or offer easy answers, he embraces mystery. He calls people into a way of living that might bring hard times, even death. What a completely different perspective than we have! Look at this passage with me:

> Dear friends, do not be surprised at the fiery ordeal that has come on you to test you, as though something strange were happening to you. But rejoice inasmuch as you participate in the sufferings of Christ, so that you may be overjoyed when his glory is revealed. If you are insulted because of the name of Christ, you are blessed, for the Spirit of glory and of God rests on you. If you suffer, it should not be as a murderer or thief or any other kind of criminal, or even as a meddler. However, if you suffer as a Christian, do not be ashamed, but praise God that you bear that name. For it is time for judgment to begin with God's household; and if it begins with us, what will the outcome be for those who do not obey the gospel of God? And, "If it is hard for the righteous to be saved, what will become of the ungodly and the sinner?" So then, those who suffer according to God's will should commit themselves to their faithful Creator and continue to do good.
>
> 1 Peter 4:12-19

Peter points to two reasons the people are suffering:
1. Because there is an enemy.
2. Because following Jesus brings hardship.

This passage is so practical, yet it is foreign to many of us. Peter was reconciling the experience of suffering for new followers of Christ. They were inclined to believe that suffering meant maybe God was punishing them, or maybe they weren't God's people after all. Sound familiar? They wondered: If they really were God's children and he was loving and good, why would they be suffering so much because of their faith?

Not long ago I received a phone call around 11 p.m. It was one of our high school guys and he was really struggling. He apologized for calling so late. He explained that his dad had been making fun of him for believing in Jesus. His dad, a strong atheist, was really disappointed that his son would believe such nonsense. His dad had walked into this guy's bedroom about an hour earlier and started to berate him. For an hour this dad belittled his son's faith. Eventually they were both screaming at each other. "It doesn't seem worth it, and maybe my dad is right," this incredible young man said to me on the phone that night.

Honestly, that's real hardship! Sure, it's not burning at the stake, crucifixion, or even what Christians are going through in parts of the world right now. But he was really hurting and confused. Just like the people Peter was writing to in the Bible, he was surprised that even after entering into a relationship with Jesus, he still had problems.

Many people today, as they have throughout history, wonder why God lets bad things happen to good people. The early Christians lived in a culture that was averse to their faith, showing little sympathy for them and their beliefs. A lot of us can relate to that.

Peter wrote about suffering because it was pivotal for new, and most likely young, followers of Jesus to understand, just as it is for us today. Peter offered them a countercultural viewpoint of suffering, one that the current overriding culture, philosophies, and religions could not supply. Suffering, he explained, is a part of growing in your faith— and suffering does not have the final word.

There are a few topics the Protestant church does not address very well. One of them is singleness, and another is what we're talking about right now, suffering. The American Dream has so supplanted the kingdom of God in our thinking that many pastors teach a false paradigm within which to practice Christian faith. The truth is, though, that suffering always has been and always will be a cornerstone to deeper intimacy with Christ. When we suffer, we identify with Jesus in his sufferings.

Just as we must have a theology of new life and healing, we must also embrace suffering and somehow hold those two ideas together so that when times get tough, we don't fall, and we don't give in to believing poor characterizations of who God is. Peter understood that, and did a brilliant job of relocating suffering within a better story.

A while ago my daughter went through a period of extreme anxiety. It got so bad that she would hear what sounded like a loud train at full steam running in her mind. I held her as she cried. It was a daily grind for quite a few years. Not long ago I had her speak to our middle schoolers. She spoke to them about the mind and about giving Christ your thoughts and allowing him to reign in your thinking. She spoke about her struggle with anxiety and how those years, when my wife and I journeyed with her, brought us closer. During that time we pursued Jesus together, even when it was hard. I couldn't believe the wisdom and clarity she spoke with. I knew we were giving our teenagers a proper view of this life, a sense of God as Immanuel—God with us. God goes *with* us through the storm. My daughter even said she was grateful for the struggle—that she found God in a more intimate way than if she never had suffered at all.

If you read and learn about the early church, you'll discover that what drew many into the movement was the way Christians were handling suffering. Their surrounding culture was not compassionate toward anyone, much less this new sect of Jewish Christ followers. To this surrounding culture, the early Jewish Christ followers were strange and different, easily blamed for whatever ailed the citizenry. They suffered at the hands of the rulers—really suffered, both physically and emotionally. At times their very lives were at stake.

Sometimes we in the West are so far removed from this kind of suffering at the hands of the powerful that we grow complacent and self-reliant. These early Christians did not have that luxury. There was also personal suffering, as the apostle Paul indicates by mentioning the thorn in his flesh in some of his writings. This is where many of us can relate, to some extent. It's hard to find a young person today who does not have at least one major debilitating thorn in their flesh. Our circumstances may look different from the early believers', but as broken and suffering individuals trying to reconcile the idea of a loving God with the incredibly painful circumstances of our lives, we share a common concern.

The way suffering is viewed by the culture is significant. You see, Peter wrapped the creator God around suffering. Many of us believe that when there is pain, discomfort, or suffering, it's evidence that there isn't a God or that he isn't a God of love. But Peter and these early followers of Jesus saw it completely differently. Jesus told them that they would suffer if they followed him. They knew that to forge ahead and to bring true change to the world would require blood, sweat, and tears. Suffering for them was evidence that the world was broken and their involvement in that brokenness was necessary. This is the polar opposite of the popular philosophies of the day, which embraced blind fate as the dictator of life. If fate is in control of your destiny, then life is not ordered and it has no meaning. If fate is blind, then this chaos and pain we experience is created by an impersonal entity, wholly uninterested in you. But if there is a creator, a God who put things together with intention, then there is order over chaos and meaning in life. A faithful creator (I Peter 4:19) is one in whom we can place our trust. If I "suffer according to God's will," there is no room for "blind fate" to influence my life as though I'm a paper boat being tossed around on the ocean. Instead there is meaning to suffering, and even as we experience it we are headed in a good direction.

If we understand that suffering is the result of evil and sin, not caused by God, we begin to get a glimpse of the complexity of it all. We begin to see that God can use evil and transform it into something good for humanity and all of creation. That's what it means for God to be sovereign—that despite evil's best efforts, God can take it and eventually raise up beauty from it.

Some of the greatest evidence for this is the evil and injustice of Jesus's death. Jesus was wrongly convicted, without representation, and then beaten and murdered on a gory cross. And yet somehow his death is the most lavish display of God's great love for us, the best thing that could have happened to us in time and eternity! There's mystery to be embraced here.

Or even look at Paul's thorn in the flesh words in 2 Corinthians 12: *in my weakness God's grace is sufficient.* There's meaning to all of this in God's economy. He uses our suffering for good and for a purpose. He redeems all things, if we allow him to.

So back to that phone call. It's now about 11:15 p.m. and I'm exhausted, hearing this young man describe the pain he feels because of his father. I listen prayerfully. I whisper under my breath, "God, give me your words."

Then he says, "Brock, can you help me?"

"I'm just so proud of you," I say. "This is really hard and I'm so glad you called. The incredible thing is that the Scriptures tell us to expect suffering when we say yes to Jesus. We are supposed to expect suffering from a world that sees Christian faith as foolishness. Your dad sees this whole thing as foolishness. But God, he is going to use this. He was with you and he doesn't want this to destroy you. He even put it in your heart to call me—he doesn't want you going through this alone, and he's going to take all of this pain and he's going to bring something really good out of it, something deep and beautiful that can be used to help others. God didn't cause this, but he will take our pain and use it to wake us up. When we struggle, we become awakened to the craziness of our self-sufficiency. We wake up to our utter need for the God who was actually with you in your bedroom as your dad was yelling at you. Jesus went into the depths of suffering on the cross, and when you suffer for Jesus—which is what you just experienced—there is never anything more intimate with God than that."

Pray, and let God worry.

–Martin Luther

15 | FRUSTRATED

I love skiing and snowboarding. It brings me spectacular joy! Once, when I was snowboarding at Big Bear Mountain with my good friend, Bob, we somehow got separated. We eventually found each other at the infirmary, each holding one arm. Both of us had caught too much air and landed on our shoulders. They gave us each a sling and some aspirin and sent us on our way. My shoulder has never been the same.

Last week, Kelsey sent me on a ski day by myself for my birthday. Now, I know for some people that might not sound too awesome, but for me it really was. She reserved a nice hotel room, mostly for her to work in while I skied. I love skiing. I love it so much that I even enjoy it by myself. It feels like a retreat to me. I put my favorite music on my headphones and head down the mountain. It's the absolute best!

But this trip started bad from the get go. First, I waited until the last minute to pack. Normally this is not a problem for me, but when I went to grab my ski equipment shortly before leaving for the mountain, I couldn't find anything. No goggles, no ski pants, no jacket, no gloves—nothing! We moved last year and somehow it got misplaced. I was ticked off, to say the least.

I ran out to get new gear at one of my favorites stores, Target. It was February, ski season. Finding winter gear should have been easy. But they had nothing for me. So then I ran to Walmart, only to strike out there as well. *I need to go into a true sporting goods store,* I thought. But the one I tried also had nothing I needed. It was a conspiracy, I swear.

I ended up going to sports superstore REI. They had what I was looking for, but here's the problem with REI: It's super expensive. It feels especially expensive when you're buying something you know you already have, but you can't find. I spent way too much money buying all new gear. Then we headed out to the mountain.

Once we finally got to the hotel, I grabbed my gear and left Kelsey to do her thing while I headed for the slopes. That's when I realized something else. I'd brought my skis, which I had been able to find at home, but had forgotten my poles and boots. I ended up spending an extra hundred bucks for rentals. Ugh! Nothing was working out. Nothing! I was fuming.

I tried to get a grip on my emotions and got on the chair lift. Immediately, the new REI goggles I'd just purchased fogged up and I couldn't see anything. Not a thing! Plus, it was snowing like nobody's business. If I took my goggles off, the snow pierced me in the eyeballs; if I kept them on, I couldn't see a thing. It was a serious catch-22. It felt even more like nothing was working. But I was determined.

I started down the mountain with about ten percent visibility. It felt dangerous and I was frustrated. I couldn't get rid of the fog on my goggles and my feet were hurting in the crappy rental boots. *But I WILL have fun, dang it!* I told myself.

I persevered for about four hours, trying to get my money's worth, but the whole time I felt frustrated. It was exhausting and everything was difficult. I was exasperated by the circumstances. I was sad that I was unable to fully enjoy the gift I'd been given as my mind continued to ruminate on all the things that weren't working the way I had wanted.

I love getting youth away from their everyday lives. I love going on retreats, camps, and mission trips. I work really hard to create environments where teenagers can experience the warmth of God. And on these trips, across the board, every time, God shows up. The way it happens doesn't look the same for everyone, but he always shows up. Our group thrives in those environments.

My least favorite part of these trips is the last day. Why? Because so many people are going back to homes and schools and relationships that are unhealthy and difficult. Their everyday lives are stifled, and it's hard to see anything good. They live in frustrating environments.

I once had a meeting with someone I worked with at my church. In this meeting she kept referring back to something I had supposedly done. I got the feeling that I had consistently bothered her. So I asked, "Do I frustrate you? It seems like this is really frustrating you." She looked at me and said, "No, you don't frustrate me, you annoy me." Ugh!

She got me thinking, but not about what I was doing that annoyed her. Instead, she got me thinking about that word, *frustrated*. Frustrated, defined in the *Merriam-Webster Online Dictionary*, means *feeling discouragement, anger and annoyance because of unresolved problems or unfulfilled goals, desires, or needs.*[21]

No matter what I attempted to change that day on the mountain, I couldn't. I couldn't fix it. It reminded me of our retreats and trips, after which so many teenagers go home to circumstances they cannot change. No matter what they do they cannot make their parents get along, or change the way their coach treats the players, or relieve the pressure school puts on students, or keep their friends from falling into self-destructive behaviors. The list could go on and on. Often, our environment back home stifles us. Our desire to change that environment is frustrated.

So what do we do? How do we come home and thrive in frustrating environments? Is it possible?

A long time ago I stopped thinking of myself as doing stuff *for* God, and instead I began to think of myself as doing things *with* God. Instead of trying to do the right things, reading my Bible, praying at the right times, being good, I decided to simply be with God, to engage in the with-ness of God. This idea works with almost all relationships, like with my wife. Kelsey wants my time and my presence more than anything else. It doesn't matter so much what we do—the main thing is being present together. It's the same with God.

As we have already looked at, God's name is Immanuel, which means God with us. Names are important. Some names have a particular significance. Adam, for example, derives from the Hebrew word *adamah,* meaning "the red soil"—suggesting something of his physical origin (Gen. 2:7). And Eve (meaning "living" or "life") was so designated because "she was the mother of all living" humans (Gen. 3:20). God changed Abram's and Sarai's names to Abraham and Sarah. In Hebrew, what is added to these names is essentially a breath mark. In other words, what God was saying to them through their new names is, "I will be closer to you than your own breath. I am with you. Every time you hear your name now, with a breath mark on the end, it will remind you of this." Names are important.

My daughter's name is Dancin. Some of our family members were embarrassed to tell their friends what we had named her. They made fun, saying, "What will you name your next kid, Prancin?!" My wife and I didn't think it was funny at the time, but it kind of was.

Her name is taken from a version of the Cinderella story. In this version, Cinderella's real name is Danielle. So we took the first part of Danielle, "Dan," and the first part of Cinderella, "Cin" and made up a new name, Dancin. We wanted her to know that she had significance and a purpose and that even when life got hard, like it did for Cinderella, she could flourish, no matter the circumstances. Cinderella faced extreme obstacles, and so do many of us. We wanted Dancin to know that she truly is a daughter of the King, a princess in the truest sense, one of God's very own. And as such, she has a calling to speak life and create beauty everywhere she goes.

Names are important. God's name Immanuel, "God with us," did not come about by accident. It actually traces back to an Old Testament prophecy about the birth of Jesus. Most other religions are about getting to God, but for followers of Jesus it's different. Our faith is about a God who comes to us, a God who is among us. His name is meant to remind us that through thick and thin, in hard or easy times, he is with us.

For much of my teen years, as I went through my day it was rare that I would even think of God. Yeah, he was there—Jesus was present in the midst of that test, game, movie, homework, hallway walk to the next class. He was with me the whole time. But I had forgotten that, and was certainly not acknowledging him. It is in our nature to forget what is good and focus on what is stressful. Our forgetfulness frustrates our efforts to live lives aware of Immanuel.

The reality is that God is not only with us, but in us. And recognizing that reality and living in it changes everything. It can even change our perspectives in extremely difficult circumstances.

Here is the reality of my day on the slopes. Toward the end of my time it just hit me out of nowhere that Immanuel was with me. And remembering that did something inside of me. I asked the God who is with me for peace. "God," I prayed, "help me to enjoy this. Help me to be aware of you."

What's strange is after praying these words, I became calm. I was sad that I had almost missed out on the joy in front of me because I could not let go of my attitude. But in that moment, in the midst of the cold, the wind, the snow, the foggy goggles, and the hurting feet, I had this overwhelming sense that God was with me. In that moment I became strong. My petty problems didn't go away, but I could bear them because I was not alone, even on the ski slopes. We are never alone. He is with us.

He who fears he will suffer, already suffers because he fears.

–Michel de Montaigne

16 | IRRATIONAL LOSS OF FEAR
PART UN

Franklin D. Roosevelt gave his first inaugural address to the nation in 1933. If you know much about American history, this was in the depth of the Great Depression and people were in the grips of fear. Fear, fed by the reality of poverty, which was coupled with a famine caused by severe drought, overwhelmed the people. Roosevelt gave a message that sounded like a sermon. He discarded his normal witty and light tone for something much more serious. The line from this address, "There's nothing to fear, but fear itself…" met citizens where they were, capturing their minds and giving them hope.

I have to confess, I have a crazy fear. Like, a really embarrassing one.

Here it is: I'm afraid of sharks. Now I know what you're thinking, "Of course you're afraid of sharks. Who isn't?!" No, you don't understand. I've been in *swimming pools* and my imagination has gotten the best of me. I'll be swimming in the pool, playing and having a good time, when all of the sudden, I'll hear it. The music from *Jaws* starts up:

"DU, DUM. DU, DUM." Can you hear it? My imagination takes over, and in a panic, I'll swim my tail off over to the side and launch my body out of the pool like a torpedo. Ridiculous, I know.

It's interesting to look at the collective fears of a community or a nation. Some, like the fears of people in the midst of the Great Depression, are rational and understandable. Some, like the fear of sharks in swimming pools, are not. But I have to tell you something: Christians should be the least fearful people on the planet.

The Scriptures tell us that there is a "great cloud of witnesses" observing us from heaven. Those who have gone before us are watching the narrative of history unfold. They are watching what we do. These mighty followers of Jesus, many of whom gave up their lives for the sake of Christ, are watching. I wonder if they watch us with shocked expressions, asking, "Why are they so afraid? What are they thinking? Don't they know who they are?"

People are born with only two fears. The first is the fear of falling and the second is the fear of noise. And these fears protect us. The fear of falling keeps us away from the edge of the cliff. Noise can alert us that something is wrong. Both of these fears are meant to keep us safe— not all fears are bad. Researchers have discovered, for instance, that monkeys, apes, and baboons have an innate fear of snakes from a very young age—as they should, and so should you. (People who carry large snakes around their necks are extremely odd to me. Maybe even more strange are the people who walk up to them and want to pet these snakes. I'm sorry, but snakes were never meant to be petted. That is disturbing. At a music festival one time a guy walking around with a huge snake around his neck asked me, "Hey, do you want to touch it?" I not-so-politely declined his offer.)

It's healthy to have some fear in your life. The problem is when the list of fears starts to grow until it leaves you stuck or incapacitated. Many of our fears are not healthy and verge on irrational. An irrational fear is a fear of something that is not likely to happen but that grips your imagination nonetheless. In other words, an irrational fear is fearing something that isn't a threat, at least not in the moment.

Take spiders, for example. You might be afraid of spiders. Just reading the word *spider*, you're kind of freaking out, aren't you? Have you ever fought with your mom over who is going to kill the spider? An itty bitty spider that you could easily crush with your pinky? That's an irrational fear. (Wouldn't it be funny if as you are reading this chapter a spider bites you? Oh my gosh, if this happens you must let me know!)

Whether they are rational or not, the question is, how do we get rid of fears that render us useless to this movement God is calling us into?

We often struggle with fear because of our experiences. Maybe when you were little you had a bad experience with water and now you're deathly afraid of it, even when the water is shallow. Maybe a parent had a fear and you picked it up from watching them, or you saw a movie about something that's plagued you ever since.

The other way that fear can latch onto us is through societal and cultural cues. I did a survey of sorts at my youth group, asking our teenagers what they were afraid of. I posed it like this: "What fears plague you in an ongoing way?" Here's what they came up with:

1. Fear of what people think of them
2. Fear of being alone and rejected
3. Fear of the future (this one seemed connected to school success and relationships)
4. Fear of failure—especially of letting people down (friends, teachers, coaches, and parents)
5. Fear of a mass shooting

If you compare this against America's collective top fears, my youth group is pretty spot on. These are our cultural fears. You may even have a couple of these yourself.

Last year I was invited by World Vision and the 30 Hour Famine to see what they were doing in Kenya. Our guide told me that a Kenyan's biggest fears are of elephants destroying their crops and wildebeests attacking them. I have to say that those two fears are not even on my radar. We live in a very different world than my Kenyan friends.

Here's the thing about fear. Someone could look deep into your eyes and say, "You do not need to be afraid of sharks in the pool, that's irrational." You would never say to them in response, "Oh thank you wise person. I never knew that. Now I will stop being afraid of sharks in the pool. Thank you so much for this valuable information."

No! We can't simply will away our fears.

There is a connecting theme that runs through all types of fear that people smarter than myself were able to identify. They have pinpointed that most fear is based on the idea of loss. We only fear something because, if it happens, we will lose something. The three most significant losses they have found are:

Loss of control
Loss of reputation
Loss of life

When we fear, we are trying to control loss. That's often what anxiety is. We try to mitigate loss by thinking about our fears and how to keep that thing from happening by analyzing *every.single.angle.* And that, my friend, is exhausting.

It's because of this that when we are afraid, we often don't act or think rationally. We apply to a million schools we know people think highly of because we are afraid of a loss of reputation if we don't. We need to get into that certain school and be seen as a success. Our parents feel similar feelings and we want to live up to their expectations. We get caught up in trying to make sure our reputations are stellar and that nothing gets in the way of their/our plans for our lives.

With the advent of social media, the weight put on the opinion of others has shifted dramatically to front and center. We are unhealthily concerned with what others think of our posts, our pictures, and our well-curated lives. Other people's opinions are everything.
But here's the deal. Christians, when they are more consumed with

Jesus's reputation than their own, when they are more concerned with living God's plan rather than all the plans they've laid out for themselves, live more satisfying and fulfilling lives.

Remember, one thing we're talking about in this book is how Christians are different. And it's true—we are different. We're the crazy ones. A good and wonderful kind of crazy. And nowhere is that more true than when it comes to fear. The early followers of Jesus actually had an irrational *loss* of fear. We should learn from these people.

Irrational Loss of Fear

One of the most significant attributes that made the early church look crazy to everyone around them was this irrational loss of fear.

People started persecuting Christians pretty early on because they were a threat to the Roman Empire. Christians wouldn't sacrifice to the Roman gods and they went around saying that Jesus, not Caesar, was Lord. They were collecting new converts daily because of how dang nice they were, caring for people who were sick and poor, feeding people, taking in orphans, and letting pretty much anyone in on this secret sauce that made them so attractive. The early church was a quickly growing and organized group of people who did not fit into the nice little categories the Roman government was comfortable with. What these early Christians were doing was seen as a full-on rebellion against the culture and against Caesar. And so the Roman Empire wanted to squash the movement. The followers of Jesus were ostracized, kicked out of their families, and their businesses were all shut down. Not only that, they were being killed *en masse*.

And here's the strange thing: The more of them that were killed, the more these radical Jesus followers grew in their faith in Jesus. Their faith kept getting stronger and stronger.

A historian (as seen in Diognetus 5:10–17) at the time described Christians this way:

> Christians obey the established law; indeed in their private lives

they transcend laws. They love everyone, and by everyone they are persecuted. They are unknown, yet they are condemned; they are put to death, yet they are brought to life. They are poor, yet they make many rich; they are in need of everything, yet they abound in everything. They are dishonored, yet they are glorified in their dishonor; they are slandered, yet they are vindicated. They are cursed, yet they bless; they are insulted, yet they offer respect. When they do good, they are punished as evildoers; when they are punished, they rejoice as though brought to life. By the Jews they are assaulted as foreigners, and by the Greeks they are persecuted, yet those who hate them are unable to give a reason for their hostility.[22]

Another example of this irrational loss of fear was observed during the spread of the plague in Rome from 250-270 AD. While most people who could fled the city, the Christian population stayed. Even though Emperor Decius blamed Christians for the plague and persecuted them throughout the empire, they remained. Among them people were dying from the disease just like everyone else, but they felt a higher calling to care for the sick and dying. Christians baffled everyone! Other people didn't know what to do with them. These early Christians had lost their fear of death, their fear of loss of control, and their fear of loss of reputation.[23]

> For to me, to live is Christ, to die is gain.
> Philippians 1:21

What would it look like to live a life where all irrational fear is gone? Where you decide to trust in God, no matter what? I bet people around you would think you were crazy irrational to live like that, just walking in God's peace and trusting him along the way. Not like some flake with no direction, but like David in the Psalms. At times you're screaming, "God, where the heck are you!" (Psalm 86) But then you're also reminding yourself that he is good, and he will work out all things for the good of those who are in him (Romans 8:28). He will guide you, he will lead you (John 16:13). He hasn't taken you this far to bring you back again (Philippians 1:6). Maybe you will be in the midst of massive disappointment, but then you'll open the Bible to Psalm 121:1-8 or maybe Romans 8:38 or Hebrews 4:14-16. You'll be reminded of who you are and who God really is, in the midst of pain and difficulty. Your eyes will be realigned to Jesus, whose name is Immanuel, God with us.

We started this chapter with Dwight D. Eisenhower and I'd like to end with the great reggae musician, Bob Marley. He sang about suffering and hope so often and so beautifully. In his song *Three Little Birds,* he sings of how the Father, the Son, and the Holy Spirit (the three little birds) sing hope into our hearts, into our minds, and into our souls. May we have ears to hear! In fact, why don't you go right now and take a listen to Bob's song, *Three Little Birds*, and let him sing over you.

I learned that courage was not the absence of fear, but the triumph over it. The brave man is not he who does not feel afraid, but he who conquers that fear.

–Nelson Mandela

17 | IRRATIONAL LOSS OF FEAR
PART DEUX

We were sitting on the floor in the youth room after the service ended when a teen looked at me and asked, "How do I know all of this stuff is true? And if it is true, why won't God answer my prayers?"

Now, I love it when youth start to ask the big questions. I love it because easy answers no longer suffice for this complicated world. I get excited when questions bubble up to the surface. When this happens it means they are beginning to think for themselves, and that's when they become dangerous: dangerous to small thinking, dangerous to power structures, dangerous to the enemy who wants to keep them small. They become wonderfully dangerous.

The first followers of Jesus saw Jesus raised from the dead. They knew that usually, dead people stay dead. These were not stupid people. But then about a thousand of them get to actually hang out with the risen Jesus for over a month. He starts teaching them and they begin to become strong, and fearless. This new reality begins to change everything for them. Then Jesus tells them that he is just the first of many who will live eternally. That death will no longer have the final word. Then he calls them into suffering for the cause. To join him in living a life of light in this oh-so-very-dark world. He promises them that if they follow him, they'll suffer. Heck, the time and location in which they all lived was violent and volatile. He tells them that he trusts them enough to handle it and then he says he will place his Spirit inside of them to give them what they need in the midst of this hard thing called life.

When anyone else would feel deep sadness because of difficulty, Jesus would come and gently fill them with joy.
When anyone else would naturally feel hatred because they were being abused, he would fill them with a supernatural ability to love.
When people were depleted and full of anxiety, he would fill them with his Spirit and give them the kind of peace that passes all understanding.

When others began to oppose them and ridicule them because of their beliefs, he would give them the gift of tolerance.
His Spirit would give them the ability to be gentle and full of self-control. All of these things would be the evidence that they were followers of him, that they belonged to a different kind of kingdom. He called these attributes fruit (Galatians 5:22-23).
Then he said, "Join me! It's going to be really hard at times, but I will be with you and in you."

And so these people did, and they were never the same.

Back to that night in the youth room. So I'm sitting on the floor with this guy who desperately wants to be a part of a movement but is unsure of what is real. Why? Because the world is broken. More accurately, his world is broken. Ultimately, he is struggling with his faith because God hasn't fixed everything. There is a lot that's not resolved. Why is there pain? Why is there suffering?

Those of us who weren't with Jesus right when he rose from the dead and weren't taught by him firsthand, we struggle. We struggle to believe that God is good and active.

The crazy thing is that this was not the case at all for the early followers of Jesus.

They knew the world was broken. Of course it was. It still is.

They were aware that bad things would happen to good people. They were ready for that. In fact, they were promised that if they followed Jesus and didn't fit in with culture and instead actually attempted to change things, suffering would come (Matthew 10:22).

They knew they belonged to another kingdom, the kingdom of God, that existed on this planet but was in constant conflict with the kingdom of this world. Jesus was calling them (just as he now calls us) to be the remedy to this problem, this conflict. And these early followers were pumped. They thought it was a privilege that God would actually trust them to represent and extend his reign everywhere they went. They were ecstatic that they were the ones God entrusted to be the walking, talking temples of his Spirit (1 Corinthians 6:19).

One of my favorite stories in the Bible is in Acts 5. The early followers of Jesus were going around telling everyone about the risen Jesus, even as they faced brutal treatment. They were so convinced of what they had seen, they didn't seem afraid at all. In fact, Acts tells us that thousands upon thousands of Jewish people were coming to faith in the risen Jesus. It was a full-on movement, but this created a problem for the disciples. There were also these teachers of the Law who were called Sadducees, and they got really jealous of the disciples' growing fame. Why were they called Sadducees? Because they were sad-you-see. (Sorry, had to do it.) But at any rate, a major conflict happens between the disciples and the Sadducees in Acts 5. The Sadducees bring the disciples in because they've heard they won't stop talking about Jesus, even after many threats.

Here's the account:

When they heard this, they were furious and wanted to put them to death. But a Pharisee named Gamaliel, a teacher of the law, who was honored by all the people, stood up in the Sanhedrin and ordered that the men be put outside for a little while. Then he addressed the Sanhedrin: "Men of Israel, consider carefully what you intend to do to these men. Some time ago Theudas appeared, claiming to be somebody, and about four hundred men rallied to him. He was killed, all his followers were dispersed, and it all came to nothing. After him, Judas the Galilean appeared in the days of the census and led a band of people in revolt. He too was killed, and all his followers were scattered. Therefore, in the present case I advise you: Leave these men alone! Let them go! For if their purpose or activity is of human origin, it will fail. But if it is from God, you will not be able to stop these men; you will only find yourselves fighting against God." His speech persuaded them. They called the apostles in and had them flogged. Then they ordered them not to speak in the name of Jesus, and let them go. The apostles left the Sanhedrin, rejoicing because they had been counted worthy of suffering disgrace for the Name. Day after day, in the temple courts and from house to house, they never stopped teaching and proclaiming the good news that Jesus is the Messiah.

Acts 5:33-42

This story is astounding to me. These followers of Jesus were flogged (beaten harshly), but left rejoicing. *Why?* Because this was what Jesus said would happen. If they truly followed him, they would be mistreated and they would suffer like him.

For these early followers of Jesus, their worldview radically shifted when they met the risen Jesus and when his Spirit filled them. When it shifted, they went from being focused on their own experiences and self-preservation to being focused and centered on Jesus.

When our experiences determine our beliefs, what we end up with is an erratic, up-and-down belief system. I have had life-changing experiences with God. I've seen many healings, felt his presence, have seen him work over and over again in people's lives. And yet I still forget all of this. I begin to doubt. When I rely on my experience as the center of my faith rather than on Jesus, it's a pretty shaky situation.

This is not a new story according to the Scriptures. The ancient Israelites, for instance, would see the hand of God, yet they would forget and go on to worship other gods. God would feed them in the morning with heavenly bread, provide shade with a massive cloud during the afternoon, and give them fire to keep them warm at night. The Israelites saw incredible and scary miracles, yet that was not enough to sustain their faith. It just wasn't. That doesn't mean those experiences weren't vital. But when experiences are our center, we become off balance.

When the early followers of Jesus began seeing the truth of Jesus in the Holy Scriptures and the community of faith, it brought them such strength. There was remarkable stability in this group of rebels that grew as they had experiences they knew could not have been brought on by themselves.

The early followers of Jesus got it. Jesus would be their center. They could leave behind fear and embrace whatever Jesus led them into because they understood something that maybe we do not.

The apostle Paul was one of the earliest leaders in the Christian church, and he established a bunch of communities of Jesus followers. Then he wrote a series of letters to those churches, helping them figure out how to follow Jesus in the midst of an empire that was oppressive to them. Now that they had committed their whole selves to Jesus, what would it look like to live this thing out?

One of the places that we see Paul articulate this Christ-centered worldview the best is in his letter to the Romans. So real quick background: Paul is laying out an argument that culminates in Romans 8. He's explaining what this Christ-centered worldview is really about. Let's start by looking at something from chapter 5 and from chapter 6 before we jump into chapter 8, because I don't want you to miss this.

Here it is:

> You see, at just the right time, when we were still powerless, Christ died for the ungodly. Very rarely will anyone die for a righteous person, though for a good person someone might possibly dare to die. But God demonstrates his own love for us in this: While we were still sinners, Christ died for us.
>
> Romans 5:6-8

The very first point to know about this new way of seeing the world is that it all starts with the fact that Jesus died for us in the midst of our apathy and sin. You and I don't have to clean ourselves up first. We don't need to initiate his favor and love. Not at all. It's all about God's grace—we receive his unearned and undeserved favor.

God loves you, even if you're dead set against him.
God loves you even if you are committed to being his enemy.
He loves you even if you don't care about him at all.
This is the foundational point and message of this new worldview.
We are the loved ones! We must start there.

Then Paul goes on to say this in Romans 6:

> For we know that our old self was crucified with him so that the body ruled by sin might be done away with, that we should no longer be slaves to sin—because anyone who has died has been set free from sin. Now if we died with Christ, we believe that we will also live with him.
>
> Romans 6:6-8

The second point to know about this new worldview is that not only did Jesus die for you, even though you were stuck in your sin, but the reason he died for you is so that you could be set free.
Free from a life of meaninglessness.
Free from living unaware of God.
Free from being led around by your own inclinations and appetites.
Free from the tyranny of self.
That stuff is no longer your identity. It no longer has power over you.

The old is gone and the new has come and we find life as we follow Jesus. There is freedom in the following.

Then we get to the slam dunk of Paul's argument in chapter 8:

> Therefore, there is now no condemnation for those who are in Christ Jesus.
>
> Romans 8:1

There is absolutely no fear of punishment for us. God doesn't love you depending on whether you do things right or wrong. There is nothing to be afraid of anymore if you have accepted the love, grace, mercy, forgiveness, and leadership of Jesus. And that's what Paul is building to in Romans. This is true even for those of us who are struggling to believe. We've been haunted by our doubts, but even in our doubts we have nothing to fear. In fact, we are free to question because our God is good and truth is never something to fear seeking.

If Jesus died for us before we ever did anything right, if he's changing us, giving us the power and setting us free, then there is nothing left to fear. Perfect love casts out all fear!

Paul's argument for this new way of thinking and living comes down, now, to this:

> If God is for us, who can be against us? He who did not spare his own Son, but gave him up for us all—how will he not also, along with him, graciously give us all things? Who will bring any charge against those whom God has chosen? It is God who justifies. Who then is the one who condemns? No one. Christ Jesus who died—more than that, who was raised to life—is at the right hand of God and is also interceding for us. Who shall separate us from the love of Christ? Shall trouble or hardship or persecution or famine or nakedness or danger or sword? As it is written:
> "For your sake we face death all day long;
> we are considered as sheep to be slaughtered."
> No, in all these things we are more than conquerors through him who loved us. For I am convinced that neither death nor life, neither angels nor demons, neither the present nor

the future, nor any powers, neither height nor depth, nor
anything else in all creation, will be able to separate us from
the love of God that is in Christ Jesus our Lord.

Romans 8:31b-39

Paul is directly addressing the loss of fear we were looking at in the
last chapter.

Is your reputation in shreds? Is your financial security at stake? Are
your plans all a mess? Is your life in danger? No one and nothing can
stand against you because Jesus thinks the best of you, Jesus has plans
for you, Jesus has justified you, Jesus has unfathomable love for you.
And if you die? He will greet you with open arms on the other side,
my friend!

This is the truth the early church heard from Paul.
And it was powerful.
Even when their experience told them that God was disappointed in
them.
Even when their experience told them that they were sinners, even
when they felt they weren't worthy.
Even when their experience told them that their hopeful plans were
not going to happen. Even then they knew that God had them.
They reminded themselves that those worries and concerns were part
of their old ways of thinking. Thinking like that would not cut it for
children of God. It wouldn't cut it for a group God had called to be
the light of the world. There was a new kingdom established, a new
order, a new vision for how to live now. They had to receive the truth
of it, step into it, live it.

The early church became dangerous to the existing power structures
because they were fearless. Fear no longer had a hold on them and
so the bullying Roman Empire became powerless. In fact, the empire
eventually became Christian. That's crazy to think about! And this
happened because these men and women allowed Jesus to transform
their thinking. Light overcame darkness. And Gamaliel's words from
Acts 5 became true: "For if their purpose or activity is of human
origin, it will fail. But if it is from God, you will not be able to stop

these men; you will only find yourselves fighting against God."

This needs to happen again today, in this generation. It's time for Christians to reclaim their place in the kingdom of God. It's time for light to shine and overcome darkness.

The great theologian of the twentieth century, Karl Barth, said that 'to clasp the hands in prayer is the beginning of an uprising against the disorder of the world.'

–Pete Greig, *Red Moon Rising: Rediscover the Power of Prayer*

18 | PRAY IT IN

Like I said, I'm full of hope. Not because I'm seeing teenagers who do not mess up and do not ever doubt or stumble. In fact it's not about "do nots" at all. I'm full of hope because of what I'm seeing young people *doing*. It reminds me of something I mentioned earlier that happened in England not too long ago.

A group of young people got together and were talking about how they really didn't know how to pray. They were all Jesus followers, but they weren't very good at actually connecting with him. So one of them challenged the whole group: "Hey, let's pray for the next twenty-four hours and see what happens!" You know those moments when someone throws out an idea that is so outlandish and ridiculous but at the same time seems incredibly inspired? This was one of them. "Let's divide up the next twenty-four hours and each of us take a few hours here and there."

And they did. The experience of seeking God through prayer as a group of friends for twenty-four hours was so powerful that someone threw out another insane idea. "Why stop now? Let's keep going. Let's pray nonstop for a week." So they divided up the week and kept going. Every moment of the next week was covered with prayer. About midway through the week something happened that they didn't expect: People started joining them. Their little group of friends grew as more and more people heard about it and started showing up to their space to pray. By the end of the week they realized that they couldn't stop. Too many people were being impacted. Too many young people were finding peace and joy and connection with God's Spirit. How could they quit now?

So they decided to keep going. Weeks turned into months and months turned into years and now they've been praying 24/7 for twenty years. Did you get that? Twenty years, nonstop, 24/7! And it's turned into a movement. They call themselves the 24/7 Prayer Movement, which has grown to have prayer spaces all over the world: in India, all over Europe, in Africa, in South America, and even North America. And this full-on movement was started by something as simple as a few friends who wanted to do something. This movement God is longing to birth out into the world begins with you and me.[24]

Our youth group was on a retreat this past weekend. Our teenagers were seeking the Lord with a kind of fervor that I hadn't seen for some time. They didn't even want to stop praying to go to lunch. After a while, I literally had to make them go and eat. Once they were done, they got right back to it. This makes sense to me, because when I look out at the young people I know and think about the ones I hear about from other places, what I'm seeing is that they have a deep longing for something called transcendence.

To be transcendent means to exceed the usual limits, or to extend or lie beyond the limits of all possible experience and knowledge.[25] Young people all over the world want to see God actually do something. In fact, they need him to. The world is too messed up for us to go on acting as if everything is okay. God has placed the desire for change in our hearts and, I'm telling you, it's not in vain.

What if youth groups stopped messing around? I don't mean totally, let's not get crazy—youth groups are always going to mess around. But what if they also got serious about Jesus? What if they became places where teenagers could find hope, healing, and deep friendship and receive vision for their lives? What if they were places where strategies to bring light to dark places were birthed? What if youth groups became places that actually helped the church become the church again? Just as the disciples in the original Jesus movement were young, my guess is that this thing needs to be led by you and your generation. The reason I'm writing this book is because I truly believe that Generation Z is ready. Can't you sense it? You're tired of the straw and ping-pong games at youth group, just like I am. You're longing for something transcendent. And that desire, my friend, is literally from God. He is doing a new thing and he's starting with you. Now is the time.

This makes me think of a high school freshman I knew named John who'd grown tired of the circular pattern of his life: Go on a retreat, experience the presence of God, go home, get busy, get caught up in all sorts of junk, then go on another retreat all dried out hoping to feel the Holy Spirit, repeat. He told me it felt pointless.

When you get to that place—where you recognize that what you're doing isn't leading anywhere—it's the absolute best, because it means the status quo is being challenged. You're neither hot nor cold and, let's face it, lukewarm will never cut it. When John got to that point he made a decision. He wasn't going to wait until he was older to make a difference. He knew how the stories end for people who live a half-hearted faith and he didn't want that. So he started getting up early to walk and pray every Thursday morning at his school. He started showing up twenty minutes early to youth group in order to lead a group of his friends in passionate prayer. He asked me if he and his friends could start praying for other teenagers who needed it after the talk instead of heading to small groups. He strategized how to start Bible breakfasts, little gatherings before school, where people could come together, open God's Word, and pray. What John is beginning to see is a little movement. It's not only changing his youth group. It's slowly changing his school and the community.

What is God calling you to do?

What problem are you called to solve?
What evil will you banish?
What wrong will you be a part of righting?

It's not okay for kids to be addicted.
It's not okay for Generation Z to be plagued by anxiety and fear.
It's not okay for middle school and high school students to be consumed with getting into the "right" college, or for college students to incur massive debt.

It's not okay for us to waste any more time playing church. It's time for us to actually be the church.

I love the heart of Jennifer. When she was a sophomore heading into her junior year she saw her friends dealing with anxiety all related to college. She knew what her friends were getting ready to experience stress-wise. So she asked her youth pastor if they could start a junior year track where people could come together and share hope, vision, prayer, and support for all of the pressure of that year. She said, "I don't want anyone being alone!"

I think of Craig, a teenager from my last youth group who had a heart for justice around the world, so he started a social justice club at his school. In this club they would look together at the injustices happening all over the globe. They would look at what people were doing to bring hope to hurting places and how they as teenagers could get involved. Craig also asked his youth pastor if he could drive a group of teens every week to serve lunch at the local soup kitchen.

Or how about a junior named Chris I met when I spoke at a camp. Chris is an intellectual and has wrestled with extreme doubt over the years. But through his searching, reading, and meeting with pastors he finally realized something: His heart is for the skeptic, and he sees his struggle with faith as a gift, even a calling. And here's something else that's awesome about Chris: He knows that no one becomes a follower of Jesus as the result of losing an intellectual argument. To encourage better kinds of discussions, he started a conversation for seekers using videos called Youth Alpha. Chris runs this course for skeptics and question-askers every eight weeks. He's seeing ten to twenty teenagers every eight weeks who decide to give their lives to Jesus. Why? It started because Chris felt compelled to actually do something for people who couldn't seem to get there intellectually.

Honestly, I could go on and on.
Because I see artists who will reclaim the arts.
Future business leaders who will use money to create remedies to problems around the world.
I see future youth pastors giving vision and hope to the next generation.
There are future teachers and lawyers and doctors and politicians in Generation Z, all of whom will bring light into very dark places.

The thing is, all of this can begin now. I believe it's already beginning.

I've seen glimpses of a movement in the past, but I've been praying for the real thing for over twenty years now.

In the Scriptures is the story of Daniel, an Israelite kid who was chosen by the conquering Babylonian empire (because of his intellect, his personality, his looks, and his athletic ability) to help Babylon get Israel to submit to them. In order to do this, the empire took away everything Daniel and the others with him had that made them culturally or religiously different, attempting to brainwash these young men into becoming good Babylonian citizens. Daniel and a few friends were taught the empire's language, culture, law, religions, and philosophies. Daniel excelled at everything the Babylonians taught him. But in resistance, Daniel continued his family's custom of praying three times a day to the God of his fathers. Three times a day he headed up to the roof of his home, visible to anyone looking, and he prayed. He didn't preach, he prayed. This was not simply an act of rebellion, it was a passionate and real act of pleading to God to come and deliver his people from bondage and oppression.

In the midst of great opposition, Daniel prayed. In the midst of massive suffering, Daniel prayed. At risk to his own life, Daniel prayed. He prayed whether he sensed God or not. He prayed whether things were going terribly wrong or wonderfully right. Three times a day he prayed, and his prayers centered him. His prayers kept him close to God. His prayers gave him favor with God, and his prayers brought him massive influence. Daniel knew, in the midst of a world heading away from God, the only thing he could do was pray. And so he did faithfully.

Daniel, like you, lived in a place and time where the idea that God could actually change a school, home, city, or a culture seemed impossible. There was no way that Babylon would ever turn to God. There was no way that the king, let alone the entire population, would ever open their lives to God. That seemed ridiculous because the culture was so set against it. The captive Israelites were being brainwashed by Babylon to become good Babylonian citizens. They were being coerced into forgetting their past and their unique identity. Daniel's own people were forgetting who they were and who their God was. But Daniel believed that the impossible was possible when it came to his God. With passionate and ongoing prayer, simply having conversations with God, he remained faithful and dependent on the one true God, even in the midst of the mounting pressure and danger he was living in.

Prayer is getting involved. Prayer is an all-in action. Prayer gets us into the heart and mind of God. And prayer is a rebellion against the current, against what is, against the direction the world is going in. It's a beautiful rebellion. And Daniel's prayers led to something great. Not only did Daniel see people turn back to God, but kings with massive influence also became believers.

Three times a day a notification I set on my phone reminds me to pray. And when this happens, no matter what I'm doing, I pause and I pray. I pray for peace. I pray for freedom and connection, I pray for individual people. I pray for a revival in my youth group. I pray that God would wake up a generation to himself and that they would lead us into a movement. I pray for those reading this book right now. I pray for you. And honestly, my prayer is that you'd join me in praying, too. That prayer would be the spark of something new in you, in your friends, in your family, and in our world.

We are all longing for more. We are dying for lives worth living. We know what's happening right now isn't working. And so we pray. Together, let's pray this thing in.

Don't obey God to get things. Obey God to get God. He is your shield and your very great reward.

–Mike Pilavachi

19 | FULL OF IT

It is snowing right now. I'm sitting here at the kitchen table as I'm typing and I can't help myself—my eyes keep looking over toward the window. The neighborhood is quiet, and everything is being covered in a beautiful white blanket. It is so peaceful. Plus, school is closed! How awesome is that? We just got back from a weekend retreat with the high schoolers in my church. We had so much fun and God exceeded all of our expectations. And now we all get to rest at our homes. No school, no work. The snow is forcing everyone to slow down long enough to catch our breath. Perfect timing!

It feels like hope.

Have you ever thought of hope as something you can feel? Sometimes you can see it, like when the momentum shifts in a basketball game and all of the sudden the team that's down starts pulling back into the game. You can literally see hope out there on the floor, even in the stands.

Of course, you can also sometimes see hope slipping away. At times it's simply a feeling, but other times it's visible.

Watching our teenagers pouring their hearts out to each other all weekend, worshiping God together with all of their might, praying for one another, sharing in barrels of laughter—it was literally a weekend of hope. And I'm full of it.

People around the country ask me to come to youth worker events and churches and youth camps to talk about this generation. Many end up surprised by my hopeful tone when I speak. Why? Because I'm so literally full of it!

I know the stats. I see the issues. I get the desperate phone calls from parents. I know what's going on. But I also get to see your generation firsthand. All over the country, teenagers are ripe for a movement. They are dying for lives worth living. They see that what's happening isn't working. They are ready! And that's all God needs.

> For I am about to do something new.
> See, I have already begun! Do you not see it?
> I will make a pathway through the wilderness.
> I will create rivers in the dry wasteland.
> Isaiah 43:19 (NLT)

On Friday night after our first program on one of our retreats, a girl named Jenna came up and asked if she could talk with me. We sat down together in the program room and she explained how she'd been so full of doubt lately that she couldn't focus. She felt frustrated as everyone else seemed to be connecting with God during worship, but for her it felt empty. She said that she'd been so busy and life had been so difficult that she'd recently been making really bad decisions, and God seemed very far away.

Here's the thing. As we talked, it felt like hope. Oh, I know it didn't *look* like hope, but there was something behind her words and tone. I knew God wanted to do something inside of her heart and mind. I knew he would honor her longing for truth and connection.

Remember Thomas? Everyone else had seen the empty tomb and had seen the risen Jesus. Everyone else had a transformative experience when Jesus showed up and revealed himself to them. But poor Thomas, he was still in his hopelessness. He was still mourning the death of Jesus, his best friend and leader. He knew dead people stay dead. There was no hope. Zero. And so when he met up with his friends and they were throwing a party, he couldn't believe it.

I can picture him now. He feels hopeless but he walks into a room of hope. Like, "What in the world, are you people drunk!?"

He asks them, "What's going on in here!?"

"Oh dude, you missed it," his friends say. "Jesus is alive! He is the Christ, the promised one. He said he would rise in three days and he did. He literally just left. You barely missed him."

Thomas is in disbelief. "No way!"

Let's remember something here: Thomas was a radical. He believed in the mission of Jesus. In fact, he was willing to die with Jesus. Remember, in the book of John, Thomas shows his commitment level:

> Then Thomas (also known as The Twin) said to the rest of the disciples, "Let us also go [with Jesus], so that we may die with him."
> John 11:14-18

Thomas was all in! In John we see that he knew that if they headed with Jesus to Jerusalem, Jesus could be crucified. Every other disciple was telling Jesus not to go back. But Jesus knew Jerusalem was exactly where he needed to be; Jesus knew his purpose. Jesus also knew his death wasn't the end of the story. In fact, he kept telling the disciples what was going to happen. Still, though, they didn't understand.

When Thomas realized they were not going to change Jesus's mind, he was ready to continue to follow him, even if it meant his own death. He was prepared and ready to die with Jesus. That's why he said they should go with Jesus, despite the danger.

I can imagine them all heading to Jerusalem, with pits in their stomachs. Maybe they even felt hopeless: *There's no way we're getting out of this.*

What's so cool about this story is that they get to Jerusalem and the first thing Jesus does is give a little glimpse of what is to come. He raises their friend Lazarus from the grave. Lazarus has been dead for four days. Four long days of hopelessness. Four days in the ground. Four days of death. When Jesus is nearby, there is always hope. Expect the unexpected.

Lazarus comes out of the tomb and the disciples cannot believe their eyes. This is hopelessness turned on its head in a matter of seconds. Lazarus, who was dead, is alive. What? He was dead for four days but now he's walking around and talking and eating. Dude, it's time to party! They celebrate—the wine is flowing and the music is pumping and people are on cloud nine.

And then, about a week later, Jesus is the one who is in the tomb. And the disciples knew this would happen! They knew that if they went to Jerusalem these frauds would kill him.

Jesus is murdered. And three days later Thomas walks into a party—a party even more epic than Lazarus's no-longer-dead party. Peter is up front leading a call and response on the mic, "You say death, I say no!" "Death!" "No!" "Death!" "No!"

Thomas can't believe what he's seeing. "What the heck is going on?!" he yells.

"Jesus rose from the dead. He's alive! He did what he said he would do!" everyone yells in crazy unison.

"What? Are you guys drunk! Are you insane? No way! I won't believe it! I can't believe. I have to see him in the flesh. I need to touch him and talk to him! I need to see him with my own eyes!"

What a prayer! What a glorious prayer! "I need to see him for myself!"

To some, this sounds like doubt. To me, it's hope. Sometimes you can't see hope, but you sure can feel it. On Friday Jesus was dead, but this was now Sunday.

Sunday morning of that same retreat, Jenna came up to me again. We had officially wrapped up that morning's worship time, but the teenagers at the retreat didn't want it to stop and so prayer and worship continued for hours. People were praying for each other and seeking God and repenting, and God was doing what he does best: Restoring. Healing. Convicting. Visioning. Hoping.

It was no longer Friday. It was Sunday and Jenna knew it. She was longing for an encounter with Jesus. She was longing for something more. Only a couple of days prior Jesus was dead to her. But now he was alive and she was ready, ready for whatever he was asking her to do. It's amazing to me how God works in so many ways. Jenna showed up fried from how she was living, but once she made room for God's people and opened herself up, God's presence broke through and met her right where she was.

She knew she'd been living basically like an atheist. Oh, she believed in God, or at least she thought she might. Be she was living as if he was dead. She rarely was aware of him. Rarely thought of him. But now, she knew. She knew there was hope.

We know what happened next. Thomas was one of about a thousand who saw Jesus raised from the dead, and he never forgot it. Remember, he's the one who was ready to die for Jesus in Jerusalem, but that wasn't Jesus's plan for him. Thomas would get the privilege of dying for Jesus, only it would be in India, and it would be later. And it wouldn't happen until after he'd carried the message of Jesus into that place. When Thomas was killed, hope didn't die with him. Thomas helped plant seven churches before he was murdered in India. Seven churches that would continue the movement. To this day Jesus is alive and well in that part of India.

Hope.
It's a funny thing, isn't it?
But when I stand in front of this generation, it's the only thing I feel.
Oh, I see the confusion.
I see the pain.
I see the addiction.
I see the stress.
I see and hear it all.
But to me, it looks like hope.

See, you're full of it.

As this book comes to an end, let me tell you what can't come to an end: the idea of God's hope for a generation, for a nation, and for a worldwide movement. Let that movement begin in us! Let it begin now.

And I promise, it will come. It will come quickly, because it is the very heartbeat of God. It is his dream and he is placing that thing inside of you and me.

Contact Brock

Brock would love to hear from you! He would love to know how God is working in your life and how this book is sparking a movement inside of you and your friends. You can find out more about him at brockmorgan.com and email him at brock@generation514.com. You can also connect with him on Instagram: @realbrockmorgan.

Additional Resources

To dive further into the ideas presented in *Beautiful Rebellion*, check out the downloadable companion curriculum written by Brock Morgan and Kelsey Morgan, available at theyouthcartel.com. For other cool extras, check out the book's website: www.beautifulrebellionbook.com.

Brock is also the author of *Youth Ministry 2027*, a fresh take on the future of youth ministry and what it means for us today that serves as both a wake-up call and an encouraging word for the path forward.

ENDNOTES

1 Kevin Reynolds, dir. *Robin Hood Prince of Thieves*. 1991. Warner Bros. Home Video, 2009 (extended version). Blu-ray Disc.

2 Gary Ross, dir. *The Hunger Games*. 2012. Lionsgate Home Entertainment, 2012. Blu-ray Disc.

3 Andy Wachowski and Larry Wachowski, dirs. *The Matrix*. 1999. Warner Bros. Home Video, 1999. DVD.

4 Steven Spielberg, dir. *Ready Player One*. 2018. WarnerBrothers, 2018. Blu-ray Disc.

5 Ron Howard, dir. *Solo: A Star Wars Story*. 2018. Lucasfilm, 2018. DVD.

6 "Stress in America: Generation Z," *American Psychological Association* (online), October 2018: https://www.apa.org/news/press/releases/stress/2018/stress-gen-z.pdf.

7 Katrina Trinko, "Gen Z is the loneliest generation, and it's not just because of social media," *USA Today* (online), May 3, 2018: *https://www.usatoday.com/story/opinion/2018/05/03/gen-z-loneliest-generation-social-media-personal-interactions-column/574701002/*.

8 "35 Generation Z Statistics to Start Building the Future of Your Brand," *99Firms.com* (online), April 23, 2019: https://99firms.com/blog/generation-z-statistics/.

9 Jared Boucher, "Top Gen Z Statistics from 2018," *The Center for Generational Kinetics* (online), https://genhq.com/top-10-ways-gen-z-is-shaping-the-future/.

10 "Jonathan Haidt The Coddling of the American Mind," YouTube video, 8:30, "Real Time with Bill Maher," October 26, 2018: https://www.youtube.com/watch?v=tKW3vKpPrlw.

11 Kelly Posner, "Preventing Suicide: Teen deaths are on the rise, but we know how to fight back," *USA Today* (online), February 7, 2018: https://www.usatoday.com/story/opinion/2018/02/07/preventing-suicide-teen-deaths-rise-but-we-know-how-fight-back-kelly-posner-column/305206002/.

12 This is a resource that I've found helpful in understanding rebellions and their stages. Gizachew Tiruneh, "Social Revolutions: Their Causes, Patterns, and Phases," *SAGE Open* (online), Vol. 4, Issue 3, September 18, 2014: https://journals.sagepub.com/doi/full/10.1177/2158244014548845.

13 Rev. Dr. Martin Luther King Jr. "Commencement Address for Oberlin College." Commencement address at Oberlin College in June of 1965, Oberlin, Ohio. http://www2.oberlin.edu/external/EOG/BlackHistoryMonth/MLK/CommAddress.html.

14 Al Aronowitz, "Chapter 2: St. Jack," *The Blacklisted Journalist* (online), Column 22, June 1, 1997: http:/www.blacklistedjournalist.com/column22.html. 15 "The Alternative Jesus: Psychedelic Christ," *Time Magazine*, Vol. 97, No. 25, "The Jesus Revolution," June 21, 1971.

15 "The Alternative Jesus: Psychedelic Christ," Time Magazine, Vol. 97, No. 25, "The Jesus Revolution," June 21, 1971.

16 Alina Tugend, "Who Benefits from the Expansion of A.P. Classes," *The New York Times Magazine* (online), September 7, 2017: https://www.nytimes.com/2017/09/07/magazine/who-benefits-from-the-expansion-of-ap-classes.html.

17 Eric Barker, "Wondering What Happened to Your Class Valedictorian? Not Much, Research Shows," *Money* (online), May 18, 2017: http://money.com/money/4779223/valedictorian-success-research-barking-up-wrong/.

18 Research Releases in Millennials & Generations, "Gen Z and Morality: What Teens Believe (So Far)," *Barna* (online), October 9, 2018: https://www.barna.com/research/gen-z-morality/.

19 Research Releases in Millennials & Generations, "Six Reasons Young Christians Leave Church," *Barna* (online), September 27, 2011: https://www.barna.com/research/six-reasons-young-christians-leave-church/.

20 Anne Lamott, *Plan B: Further Thoughts on Faith* (New York: Riverhead, 2004).

21 "frustrated." *Merriam-Webster.com*. 2019. https://www.merriam-webster.com (June 5, 2019).

22 Matthew J Thomas, "Suffering and persecution in early Christianity," *IFES* (online), May 23, 2017: https://en.ifesjournal.org/suffering-and-persecution-in-early-christianity-518e73b29d8b.

23 Candida Moss, "How an apocalyptic plague helped spread Christianity," *CNN Belief Blog* (online), June 23, 2014: http://religion.blogs.cnn.com/2014/06/23/how-an-apocalyptic-plague-helped-christianity/.

24 Learn more at www.24-7prayer.com.

25 "transcendent." *Merriam-Webster.com*. 2019. https://www.merriam-webster.com (July 22, 2019).

61048026R00106

Made in the USA
Middletown, DE
17 August 2019